PROTECTING CHILDREN AND YOUNG PEOPLE

SERIES EDITORS

ANNE STAFFORD and **SHARON VINCENT**

The University of Edinburgh/NSPCC Centre for UK-wide Learning in Child Protection (CLiCP)

CHILD PROTECTION REFORM ACROSS THE UNITED KINGDOM

Edited by

Anne Stafford, Sharon Vincent and Nigel Parton

Published by
Dunedin Academic Press Ltd
Hudson House
8 Albany Street
Edinburgh EH1 3QB
Scotland

ISBN 978-1-903765-97-5
ISSN 1756-0691

First published June 2010, reprinted November 2010

British Library Cataloguing in Publication data
A catalogue record for this book is available from the British Library

Typeset by Makar Publishing Production, Edinburgh
Printed in the United Kingdom by CPI Antony Rowe
Printed on paper from sustainable resources

Contents

About CLiCP   vi

The Contributors   vii

Glossary of Abbreviations   xi

Background and Introduction   xii

Chapter 1 An overview of safeguarding and protecting children across the UK – *Sharon Vincent*   1

Chapter 2 *Every Child Matters: Change for Children* programme in England – *Nigel Parton, Phillip Noyes and Wendy Rose*   12

Chapter 3 Children and young people: rights to action in Wales – *Jonathan Corbett and Wendy Rose*   31

Chapter 4 Our children and young people – our shared responsibility: the reform implementation process in child protection services in Northern Ireland – *John Devaney, Fionnuala McAndrew and Tony Rodgers*   45

Chapter 5 Getting it Right for Every Child in Scotland – *Maggie Tierney, Christine Knight and Anne Stafford*   62

Chapter 6 Safeguarding and protecting children across the UK: similar but distinctive systems – *Anne Stafford, Sharon Vincent and Nigel Parton*   77

References   82

Index   90

About CLiCP

The University of Edinburgh/NSPCC Centre for UK-wide Learning in Child Protection (CLiCP) is a research centre based at The University of Edinburgh. It was set up in a unique collaboration between NSPCC and the University to conduct research and provide analysis and commentary on child protection policy across the UK. Current areas of research include monitoring and tracking developments in child protection in each part of the UK, child deaths, children and domestic abuse, child protection in sport, child sexual abuse, vetting and barring, devolution, children and resilience.

Contact: 0131 651 6100

www.clicp.ed.ac.uk

The Contributors

Jonathan Corbett is Assistant Chief Inspector, Care and Social Services Inspectorate Wales. His career in social work spans 31 years. He first worked in local authority social services in Wales for eleven years before moving to work in the children's voluntary sector for nine years, where he held a number of national posts for Barnardo's, Action for Children and The Children's Society. Jonathan joined the Social Services Inspectorate in Wales as an Inspector in 1997, taking up a full-time post in the Inspectorate's children's development unit the following year. In 2003 he was appointed Deputy Chief Inspector for the children's development unit. In April 2007 the Social Services Inspectorate and Care Standards Inspectorate in Wales were merged within the newly created Care and Social Services Inspectorate Wales.

John Devaney is a Lecturer in Social Work at Queen's University Belfast. Prior to this appointment in 2006 he was the Professional Advisor to the Eastern Area Child Protection Committee and Principal Social Worker for the Eastern Health and Social Services Board. He is currently Chair of the Northern Ireland branch of the British Association for the Study and Prevention of Child Abuse and Neglect, a multidisciplinary professional association. John's current research interests lie in the areas of safeguarding children from abuse and neglect, the impact of childhood adversity on later outcomes in adulthood, and violence against the person in intimate relationships.

Christine Knight is an inspector with HMIE. She has previously worked as a teacher, an advisor and education manager.

Fionnuala McAndrew is Director of Social Care and Children in the Health and Social Care Board, established on 1 April 2009. Since 2007 she has been joint project lead for the reform of children's services across Northern Ireland. Since qualifying as a social worker Fionnuala has worked in all aspects of social care including the regulation and inspection of services. She is chair of a range of multidisciplinary and multi-agency groups aimed at ensuring more coordinated planning and delivery of services to children and families.

Phillip Noyes is Director of Strategy and Development at NSPCC. He is responsible for seven strategic themes identified in the recent NSPCC Strategy and manages all seven strategic theme leads. Prior to his appointment to this post in November 2009 he was Director of Public Policy with NSPCC where he led on education, influence and change to protect children and prevent cruelty.

Nigel Parton took up the NSPCC Chair in Applied Childhood Studies at the University of Huddersfield in 2006 and he is Honorary Visiting Professor to The University of Edinburgh/NSPCC Centre for UK-wide Learning in Child Protection (CLiCP). Prior to that he was the Professor in Child Care and Director of the Centre of Applied Childhood Studies at the University. Particular areas of interest include the political dimensions of social work; changes in child care policy and practice; the politics and practice of child protection; the background and impact of the Children Act 2004; social theory, social constructionism and social work; risk and social welfare. He has been a member of numerous research advisory groups including currently the Global Partnership for Transformative Social Work based at the University of Vermont, USA. He is also Chair of the Editorial Board of Children and Society (Blackwell in association with the National Children's Bureau) and on the Editorial Board of eleven other national and international journals in the fields of child welfare and social work.

Tony Rodgers is Assistant Director of Social Services in the regional Health and Social Care Board, Northern Ireland. From 2007 he has been joint Project Leader for the Reform Implementation Team process along with Fionnuala McAndrew. Tony has extensive experience in child and family care social services as practitioner, operational manager at various levels and as commissioner. He is committed to partnership working as chair of the Childcare Partnership and the Regional Child Protection Committee. The RIT process also operates on a multi-agency basis bringing together other stakeholders across the statutory and voluntary sectors to make a difference in children's lives.

Wendy Rose is a Senior Research Fellow at The Open University. For eleven years she was a senior civil servant in England advising on children's policy. She has a background in social work practice and social services management. She works on national and international child welfare research and development projects. She is currently a professional adviser working with the Scottish Government on its policy Getting it Right for Every Child. She has published widely on policy and practice issues concerned with improving outcomes for children and families. With Julie Barnes she undertook the second national biennial study of reviews of child deaths and serious injuries in England, *Improving Safeguarding Practice: A Study of Serious Case Reviews 2001–2003*.

Anne Stafford is Director of The University of Edinburgh/NSPCC Centre for UK-wide Learning in Child Protection (CLiCP). Previously, Anne was Deputy Director of the Centre for Research in Education, Inclusion and Diversity (CREID), also at the University of Edinburgh. She was Deputy Director of the Glasgow Centre for the Child and Society at the University of Glasgow from 2001–2004. Before that, for more than ten years, she was Head of Policy and Research for the children's organisation Children 1st. Her research focus is child abuse and child protection, children's rights, and children and young people on the margins.

Maggie Tierney joined the Scottish Government in 2000 and is currently Deputy Director of the Learning Directorate, with responsibility for the Support for Learning Division. Her previous role, until August 2009, was head of child protection policy within the Children, Young People and Social Care Directorate. Previous government roles included head of social work and social care workforce planning, and external relations policy.

Sharon Vincent is Senior Research Fellow, The University of Edinburgh/ NSPCC Centre for UK-wide Learning in Child Protection (CLiCP). She has been involved in research relating to child protection and child welfare for ten years. She worked as a researcher in the Social Work Services Inspectorate for over four years where she was a member of the team which undertook the National Audit and Review of Child Protection. She then worked as a Senior Research Officer in the Development Department of the Scottish Executive. Between 2005 and 2007 Sharon was a researcher at Barnardo's, where she worked on a number of research projects including A Process Review of the

Child Protection Reform Programme with colleagues from the University of Dundee. Since joining CLiCP in 2007 Sharon has undertaken research on child deaths and serious abuse, domestic abuse and resilience.

Glossary of Abbreviations

ACPC	Area Child Protection Committee
AYE	Assessed Year in Employment
CAFCASS	Children and Family Court Advisory and Support Service
COSLA	Convention of Scottish Local Authorities
CPC	Child Protection Committee
CSSIW	Care and Social Services Inspectorate Wales
CYPP	Children and Young People's Plan
DHSSPS	Department of Health, Social Services and Public Safety
ECM	*Every Child Matters*
GIRFEC	*Getting it Right for Every Child*
HMIE	Her Majesty's Inspectorate of Education
HSS	Health and Social Services
ICT	Information Communication Technology
JAR	Joint Area Review
LSCB	Local Safeguarding Children's Board
NSPCC	National Society for the Prevention of Cruelty to Children
Ofsted	Office for Standards in Education, Children's Services and Skills
RIT	Reform Implementation Team
SNP	Scottish National Party
SOA	Single Outcome Agreement
UNOCINI	Understanding the Needs of Children in Northern Ireland

Background and Introduction

This book provides selective commentary on the systems operating to safeguard and protect children in the four parts of the UK: England, Wales, Northern Ireland and Scotland. The origins of the book lie in a seminar organised by the The University of Edinburgh/NSPCC Centre for UK-wide Learning in Child Protection (CLiCP) in 2009. Key players in the field were invited to reflect on recent reform of and developments in safeguarding and child protection.

Each part of the UK has over the past decade introduced major programmes of reform in children's services and, in particular, in those services that safeguard and protect children. Speakers addressed issues such as the main drivers for system change, visions for reform, and methods for implementing the reform programmes. For the three devolved countries—Wales, Northern Ireland and Scotland—it was a chance to reflect on new opportunities afforded by devolution for policy development and to assess the extent to which new possibilities for developing autonomously were being realised in practice.

The book is the result of further refinement of written presentations but it remains based on the personal reflections of speakers at the seminar.

It may be useful to begin by reflecting on our reasons for having written this book. First, it fills a gap in current knowledge. The Centre for Learning in Child Protection (CLiCP), responsible for producing the book, was itself set up to track and monitor developments in child protection policy across the UK. From CLiCP's inception, it seemed clear that among academics, policy makers and practitioners there was detailed information about the system they were working in, but scant knowledge of other UK systems and little oversight of developments across the UK as a whole.

In addition, CLiCP was set up amid growing awareness that devolution was creating new possibilities for divergent policy development across the UK in relation to safeguarding and protecting children. While the possibility of divergence existed, the extent to which this has happened in practice was not well understood.

The CLiCP seminar upon which the book draws was an early attempt to bring together key child protection players to exchange information about developments in safeguarding and protecting children in the context of devolution, to consider similarities and differences between the different systems of the UK and to draw out potential points of learning from each other. The book emerged from a process of genuine dialogue between key players in child protection across the UK.

This kind of intra-country comparative work is important. It provides a wide perspective from which to consider one system in the context of other systems. This was clearly articulated at an international conference organised by the then Scottish Executive as part of Scotland's audit and review of its child protection system in 2002. By way of rationale for the event, one speaker highlighted the importance of comparative work in providing the opportunity to 'raise one's head and reflect on one's own system in relation to other systems', thus arriving at a deeper understanding of one's own system. The speaker quoted the famous Scottish (anti-)psychiatrist R. D. Laing who said 'Comparison allows you to unpickle yourself from your place in the pickling jar and see that there is a different kind of life' (quoted by Andrew Cooper in Hill *et al.*, 2002).

This 'unpickling' sits at the core of CLiCP's remit and is the main focus of this book. Our interest is in being able to raise our heads and learn from our near neighbours in different parts of the UK.

In Chapter 1 Sharon Vincent provides a summary overview of key elements of systems in the four parts of the UK. Looking across the main frameworks, policies and structural aspects of the different systems, she summarises key similarities and differences.

In Chapter 2, Nigel Parton, Phillip Noyes and Wendy Rose describe recent developments in safeguarding children and young people in England. They examine the major reforms introduced by the *Every Child Matters: Change for Children* (ECM) programme. They assess these changes in the context of earlier developments in child protection in England. The role of media reporting of high profile child protection cases as a mechanism for driving system change is considered and the most recent changes to the system in England following the death of Peter Connelly (Baby Peter) are set out.

Jonathan Corbett and Wendy Rose reflect on developments in services to safeguard children and young people in Wales in Chapter 3. While there are many similarities between systems for safeguarding children in Wales and England, there are also key differences. The authors reflect on policy direction being taken by the Welsh Assembly Government since devolution and on new potential to develop Wales-specific policy.

In Chapter 4 John Devaney, Fionnuala McAndrew and Tony Rodgers discuss Northern Ireland's first major reform of public services for thirty years and within this they consider developments and proposed reform of children's services and new arrangements to safeguard vulnerable children. They discuss new attempts to introduce change at an all-Northern Ireland level; and they outline the innovative ways in which change is being introduced in practice.

Maggie Tierney, Christine Knight and Anne Stafford, in Chapter 5, describe and reflect on the period of significant reform of children's services and within that of child protection reform that has occurred in Scotland since 2000. They assess the extent to which Scotland's distinctive Children's Hearing System sets it apart from other systems of the UK. The *Getting it Right for Every Child* (GIRFEC) framework currently being tested and rolled out in Scotland is considered alongside Scotland's innovative regime for inspecting child protection services.

In the concluding chapter the editors consider some broad themes that are emerging, including the general direction of change and an early assessment of what is happening to child protection across the UK in the context of devolution.

CHAPTER 1

An overview of safeguarding and protecting children across the UK

Sharon Vincent

Introduction

Services to safeguard and protect children are underpinned by complex systems of legislation, guidance, regulations and procedures. These systems are not the same in different parts of the UK. Each part of the UK has undergone considerable reform in relation to safeguarding and protecting children over the last decade, with some parts of the UK having introduced new legislation, policy and structures to better protect children, strengthen local cooperation and increase accountability.

This chapter provides a brief overview of the different approaches to safeguarding and protecting children across the UK, concentrating in particular on the recent period of reform. It compares and contrasts policies, legislation and procedures in different parts of the UK and identifies common themes as well as differences. It focuses on systems in England, Scotland, Wales and Northern Ireland, but acknowledges that approaches to safeguarding may vary in other parts of the UK, such as the Channel Islands and the Isle of Man.

Overarching children's policy and outcomes frameworks

It is not possible to separate policy and practice to safeguard and protect children from the wider policy context surrounding child welfare. Each area of the UK has a whole host of policies to safeguard and protect children and young people and promote their general well-being, and each area has its own overarching children's policy framework within which all of these various policies fit together. These frameworks are:

- *Every Child Matters: Change for Children* programme in England (HM Government, 2004);
- *Children and Young people: Rights to Action in Wales* (Welsh Assembly Government, 2004);
- *Children and Young People – Our Pledge: A Ten Year Strategy for Children and Young People* in Northern Ireland (Office of the First Minister and Deputy First Minister, 2006);
- *Getting it Right for Every Child in Scotland* (Scottish Government, 2008).

Integrating all policy in relation to children together into one overarching policy document is a relatively new phenomenon in the UK. England and Wales were the first areas of the UK to produce an integrated policy framework. *Every Child Matters* (ECM), introduced in 2004, was a response to the *Laming Report* (2003) and to *Safeguarding Children: A Joint Chief Inspectors' Report on Arrangements to Safeguard Children* (Department of Health, 2002), which had similar findings to the *Laming Report* (Frost and Parton, 2009). It was a strategy for integrated children's services to improve outcomes for all children. The ECM vision was that practice would be determined by the needs of the child, there would be a continuum of services from early needs through to child protection risks, and children and families would get a more joined up, coordinated response without the need for multiple assessments.

Children and Young People's Rights to Action in Wales was also a response to the *Laming Report*. It represents a vision for all children in Wales and is underpinned by a commitment to preventive services and early intervention. The Welsh Assembly Government has also undertaken a review of policies and practices for safeguarding vulnerable children in Wales. The Review produced a report called *Keeping Us Safe* (National Assembly for Wales, 2006).

Northern Ireland's ten-year strategy document followed a review of safeguarding that was undertaken in response to the Laming recommendations. It represents a shared vision for children and young people based on a whole child approach and includes a commitment to preventative and early intervention practice (Office of the First Minister and Deputy First Minister, 2006).

Getting it Right for Every Child (GIRFEC) followed a national audit and review of child protection in Scotland (Scottish Executive, 2002) and sub-sequent Child Protection Reform Programme. It is a common, coordinated approach across all agencies that supports the delivery of appropriate, pro-portionate and timely help to all children as they need it. In common with ECM, *Children and Young People's Rights to Action in Wales* and *Children and Young People – Our Pledge: A Ten Year Strategy for Children and Young People* in Northern Ireland, the emphasis is on prevention and early intervention. The then Scottish Executive published the original GIRFEC *Implementation Plan* in June 2006. In September 2006 five 'pathfinders' were launched to test out the GIRFEC approach in practice and help inform future national guid-ance and best practice (Stafford and Vincent, 2008). At the time of writing the pathfinder evaluation had been completed and the Scottish Government were in the process of rolling GIRFEC out across Scotland.

All parts of the UK are committed to promoting outcomes for children and young people and all of the overarching children's policy frameworks are underpinned by national outcomes. In England there are five *Every Child Matters* outcomes: to be healthy, stay safe, enjoy and achieve, make a positive contribution, and achieve economic well-being. Northern Ireland has the same *Every Child Matters* outcomes as England with the addition of 'rights'. Wales has seven core aims, developed from the principles of the United Nations Convention on the Rights of the Child: have a flying start in life; have a comprehensive range of education and learning opportun-ities; enjoy the best possible health and be free from abuse, victimisation and exploitation; have access to play, leisure, sporting and culture activities; be listened to, treated with respect and have their race and cultural identity recognised; have a safe home and a community which supports physical and emotional well-being; and not be disadvantaged by poverty. In Scotland there are eight national outcomes: safe, healthy, achieving, nurtured, active, respected, responsible and included.

Legislation

In each part of the UK policy and practice to safeguard and protect children is underpinned by legislation. There is no separate legislation for child pro-tection, rather legislation covers child welfare in a broad sense, encompass-ing support for children in need as well as children in need of protection (Lindon, 2008). Although all parts of the UK have undergone significant reform of child protection policy in recent years, legislative change has been relatively minor. The key legislation underpinning the child protection

system in all parts of the UK remains the Children Acts which were introduced in the late 1980s and 1990s. These acts define the thresholds for intervention in family life to protect children from abuse and neglect, and the
definitions of 'significant harm' and 'children in need' within these acts have
not been amended (Owen, 2009).

The key piece of legislation in England and Wales remains the Children
Act 1989, although the Children Act 2004 has amended some of the provisions of the 1989 Act. The Children Act 2004 aimed to give statutory force
to the new shared vision of a child-centred outcomes-led approach to child
welfare services within ECM, to create clearer accountability between agencies, to enable better joint working to improve children's well-being and to
secure a better focus on safeguarding children (Rose, 2009; Frost and Parton,
2009; Luckock, 2007).

> The Children Act 2004 is primarily about new statutory leadership
> roles, joint planning, and commissioning of children's services,
> and how organisations ensure their functions are discharged in a
> way which safeguards children and promotes their welfare (Owen,
> 2009, p. 17).

Section 11 imposed a duty on agencies working with children and young
people to safeguard and promote their welfare. Another significant change
is that non-statutory Area Child Protection Committees were replaced with
statutory Local Safeguarding Children Boards.

There are some differences between the application of the Children Act
2004 in England and Wales. For example, in England Local Safeguarding
Children Boards have a duty to develop child death review panels; this duty
does not apply in Wales. Since 2007 Wales has had new powers to make
their own primary legislation in relation to vulnerable children so further
divergence is likely.

In Northern Ireland the Children Northern Ireland Order 1995 remains
the primary piece of legislation in relation to the protection of children but
new legislation to introduce a Safeguarding Board for Northern Ireland to
replace Area Child Protection Committees has been proposed.

In Scotland, the Children (Scotland) Act 1995 remains the key legislation and there are no plans either to amend this or introduce further legislation. The GIRFEC reforms, as originally proposed by the previous Labour
administration, included plans for new legislation in the form of the draft
Children's Services Bill 2006. Shortly after the issue of the draft Bill there was

however, a change of administration in Scotland. The current SNP government, who came to power in May 2007, supported the GIRFEC proposals and have pressed ahead with their implementation, but are committed to doing so, at least for now, within the confines of existing legislation (Stafford and Vincent, 2008). A Concordat with local government in November 2007 heralded a new tone of facilitation between central and local government in Scotland, rather than direction from central government, and a new collaborative approach to policy development. In keeping with this the Scottish Government favours non-statutory rather than statutory guidance to Chief Officers (Vincent, 2009).

Guidance

Procedures for responding to child protection concerns are set down both in law and in related guidance. An essential plank of child protection policy in all four parts of the UK is interagency guidance for professionals who work within child protection services. Each part of the UK has its own interagency guidance. England and Wales both updated their interagency guidance following the 2004 Children Act to take account of new statutory duties within the Act. At the time of writing, in England the most up to date guidance was *Working Together to Safeguard Children* (HM Government 2006) but this was being updated; in Wales *Safeguarding Children: Working Together under the Children Act 2004* (Welsh Assembly Government, 2006c). Wales also has *All Wales Child Protection Procedures* (2008) which were produced for all Local Safeguarding Children Boards in Wales.

In Northern Ireland the latest version of interagency guidance is *Co-operating to Safeguard Children* (Department of Health, Social Services and Public Safety, 2003b), which was updated to take account of the recommendations in the *Laming Report* (2003). In Scotland interagency child protection guidance is currently being reviewed, but at the time of writing the most up-to-date guidance was *Protecting Children – a Shared Responsibility: Guidance on Inter-agency Co-operation* (Scottish Office, 1998).

Structures for planning and delivering services

In England under the Children Act 2004 every local authority must appoint a Director of Children's Services and a Lead Councillor for children and, at a minimum, merge their education departments with the children's social care section of the old social services departments. The aspiration was that local authorities would set up a Children's Trust bringing together social services, education, health and other children's services in order to facilitate integrated front-line practice, but it was recognised that the nature and pace of change would vary. Statutory Local Safeguarding Children's Boards have wider responsibilities for the safeguarding of children than their predecessors, the non-statutory Area Child Protection Committees which had a much narrower child protection focus. These are key mechanisms for agreeing how relevant organisations will cooperate to safeguard and promote the welfare of children and for ensuring the effectiveness of what these organisations do (O'Brien *et al.*, 2006). The decision to place LSCBs on a statutory footing and create Directors of Children's Services responsible for ensuring their effectiveness was a response to Lord Laming's recommendation that there should be a line of accountability from front-line services through to government. The Children's Trust has a wider role than the LSCB in planning and delivery of children's services. All local areas must produce a Children and Young People's Plan (CYPP) and LSCBs contribute to and work within the framework established by the CYPP (Vincent, 2008b).

In Wales, as in England, all local authorities are required to produce a CYPP but structures in Wales are slightly different from those in England. Wales does not have Children's Trusts. Education and social care are not integrated, and local authorities are still required to have Directors of Social Services. Wales does, however, have Children and Young People's Framework Partnerships, made up of local authority and health services and the voluntary sector. Children and Young People's Framework Partnerships are responsible for developing the Children and Young People's Plan and for driving the commissioning of services. The Children Act 2004 contained specific clauses for Wales making it a legal requirement to set up Children and Young People's Framework Partnerships in all local authority areas. As in England, statutory Local Safeguarding Children's Boards replaced non-statutory Area Child Protection Committees under the Children Act 2004.

Northern Ireland has somewhat different structures. Unlike the rest of the UK, local authorities in Northern Ireland do not have primary responsibility for planning and delivering children's services. Instead this is the function of joint Health and Social Services (HSS) Boards. Each HSS Board is required to produce a Children's Services Plan. Northern Ireland has Area Child Protection Committees in each HSS Board whose role is to determine the strategy for safeguarding children and to develop and disseminate policies and procedures. In addition each Health and Social Services Trust has a Child Protection Panel to facilitate practice at a local level. There are, however, proposals for a new single statutory Safeguarding Board for Northern Ireland which will have responsibility for strategic matters and five Safeguarding Panels, one in each joint Health and Social Services Trust, which will have a coordinating and operational role. These new arrangements represent a widening remit from traditional child protection responsibilities to broader safeguarding responsibilities as in England and Wales (Vincent, 2008b).

In Scotland, the way in which local child protection services are structured varies. There are a few integrated children's departments, but most local authorities have retained Directors of Social Work. As in other parts of the UK, local authorities have responsibility for producing an integrated children's services plan. Scotland has non-statutory Child Protection Committees which are responsible for the strategic planning of local interagency child protection work and there are no plans to replace them with statutory bodies. However, under guidance issued as part of the Child Protection Reform Programme (Scottish Executive, 2005), the responsibilities of Child Protection Committees have been broadened and accountabilities strengthened. As a result CPCs now have a broader remit. They no longer have a narrow child protection focus and are, therefore, comparable to Local Safeguarding Children Boards in other parts of the UK (Vincent, 2008a; 2008b).

The child protection system in Scotland is also different from that in other parts of the UK because of the unique Children's Hearing System. While concerns about children are dealt with by social work departments and the police as they are in other parts of the UK, a referral must be made to the Children's Hearing if compulsory measures may be needed. Anyone, not just professionals, can contact a Children's Reporter if they have concerns about a child (Stafford and Vincent, 2008).

Processes and procedures

Legislative grounds for intervention define the circumstances and the threshold at which the statutory child protection system is legally required to intervene to protect a child. Legislation and guidance in all parts of the UK stipulate that if statutory services have reasonable cause to suspect that a child is suffering, or likely to suffer, 'significant harm' then they have a duty to make child protection enquiries. Interagency guidance outlines the procedures for handling individual cases. The broad stages of the process— referral, investigation and assessment, case conference and case management and review—are the same in each part of the UK but within these broad stages there are some distinctive features (Vincent, 2008a).

In all four parts of the UK the child protection process begins when someone—a professional, a family member, a child, or a member of the public—expresses concern about the welfare of a child. Concerns may be communicated as a referral to statutory services: the social work department or Children's Reporter (Scotland); social services (Northern Ireland); local authority children's social care (England and Wales); or the NSPCC in England, Wales or Northern Ireland. Referrals, which are normally made by telephone, are screened by statutory agencies. In Northern Ireland guidance states that telephone referrals should be followed up in writing within 24 hours; in England and Wales within 48 hours (the Scottish guidance does not specify that referrals should be followed up in writing).

Initial investigation is undertaken by a social worker, or in Scotland by a Children's Reporter, to determine whether the case meets legislative grounds for intervention. Information may be gathered by undertaking an initial assessment. Referrals may result in a number of different routes being taken including no further action, referral to another service for family support if the child is considered to be in need but not at risk of significant harm, or further investigation. Where the concern may constitute an offence the police must be informed.

Sometimes emergency action will need to be taken to protect the child. Emergency procedures to protect children who are believed to be in immediate danger exist in all four parts of the UK and may be invoked at any point in the child protection process. All four areas of the UK have Emergency Protection Orders (known as Child Protection Orders in Scotland), Exclusion Orders and police protection powers. The guidance in England, Wales and Northern Ireland stipulates that whenever there is reasonable cause to suspect a child is suffering significant harm, or likely to suffer significant harm, a strategy discussion involving social care or social services, the police and other appropriate agencies should be initiated by social care or social services at the earliest opportunity. The Scottish guidance states that other agencies should be consulted but does not specifically refer to a 'strategy discussion'.

Once it has been decided that a child may have suffered, or is at risk of suffering, significant harm, social work, social services or local authority children's social care need to undertake a joint investigation with the police. In England, Wales and Northern Ireland the NSPCC also has the power to investigate and in Scotland Children's Reporters. Assessment is part of the process of joint investigation. Each part of the UK has developed tools for assessing children's needs:

- in England *The Framework for the Assessment of Children in Need and their Families* and the *Common Assessment Framework*;
- in Northern Ireland *Understanding the Needs of Children in Northern Ireland* (UNOCINI);
- in Scotland the *My World Triangle*;
- in Wales *The Framework for the Assessment of Children in Need and their Families*.

These assessment frameworks were constructed as guides to help practitioners from all disciplines organise their thinking when there are concerns about a child, and to make sense of the information they gather (Rose, 2009). There are similarities between these assessment frameworks. They all stress the importance of multi-agency assessment, acknowledging that individual practitioners will not be able to conduct a comprehensive assessment because they are unlikely to have all of the necessary information about a child. The assessment frameworks are all designed to be used to assess need; they are not only for use in child protection cases (Frost and Parton, 2009). The assessment frameworks are also alike in that they are informed by research and theory in relation to child development. They all stress that the child and family should be involved in the assessment process. If, however, parents refuse access to the child for the purpose of assessment, agencies in all four areas of the UK may apply for a Child Assessment Order.

Following initial investigation, if a child is still considered to have suffered, or to be at risk of suffering, significant harm then an initial child protection case conference may be convened. In England, Wales and Northern Ireland a case conference must be convened within 15 days of the first strategy discussion; in Scotland no timescales are specified. The case conference brings together professionals involved with the family, family members and, where they are older, the children themselves. At the conference professionals decide whether or not to place the child's name on the Child Protection Register.

If a child is placed on the register a child protection plan must be developed for the child. A core group of professionals will be identified to implement the care plan and a named professional, usually a social worker, will take responsibility for the case and be responsible for completing a comprehensive assessment of the child's needs. Since the introduction of their new Integrated Children's System England and Wales no longer have a Child Protection Register but there is registration in the sense that children are recorded as having a child protection plan. Scotland and Northern Ireland have maintained the Child Protection Register. In all parts of the UK children must be categorised under a specific type of abuse: neglect, physical abuse or injury, sexual abuse, or emotional abuse. Definitions of abuse and neglect are outlined in interagency guidance. These definitions are similar across the UK but there are some variations.

- in England and Wales the definition of physical abuse specifically mentions that a parent or carer may fabricate or induce illness in a child but this is not covered in the guidance in Scotland or Northern Ireland;
- in Northern Ireland and Wales, but not England and Scotland, the guidance specifically states that domestic abuse, parental mental health problems and parental substance misuse may expose children to emotional abuse;
- the English definition of sexual abuse specifically mentions children and young people involved in prostitution unlike the definitions in other parts of the UK;
- the English definition of neglect states that neglect may occur during pregnancy as a result of maternal substance misuse; this is not included in the definitions of neglect in other parts of the UK;
- in Scotland there is a fifth category of registration not found in other parts of the UK—non-organic failure to thrive (Vincent, 2008a).

In all areas of the UK child protection case conference reviews take place three months after the initial conference and then at six-month periods if the child remains on the register and/or continues to have a child protection plan. A child's name will be removed once they are considered to be no longer in need of a child protection plan because the reasons for registration no longer apply (Lindon, 2008).

Conclusion

There are significant differences in structures, policies and services to safeguard and protect children across the UK, but there are also many parallels and all parts of the UK approach safeguarding and child protection in broadly similar ways. What we have seen across the UK in recent years is not a radical overhaul of policy and practice to protect children, rather a refocusing of services (Luckock, 2007). All parts of the UK have retained the core elements of a forensic investigative model of child protection. Formal child protection systems and procedures have remained relatively unchanged with most reform being focused around the early intervention stage of the process. The policy emphasis across the UK has been one of prevention and early intervention. The idea is that children's needs can be assessed and addressed at an early stage in order to prevent escalation further down the line. The development of new integrated assessment frameworks plays a major role in this. Integrated assessment frameworks are part of a general strategy to refocus children's services so that they are more broadly based to meet the needs of vulnerable children and their families (Rose, 2009). There has been an emphasis across the UK on integrating services. Instead of separating services for children at risk from services for children in need, the emphasis is on identifying the needs of all children and integrating services around these needs. Policy has become more child focused and the well-being of all children is the outcome to be achieved (Luckock, 2007; Frost and Parton, 2009).

Across all four parts of the UK child protection is no longer just about children at the hard end of the system. The direction of policy has moved from a narrow child protection focus on children who have been abused and neglected towards a wider focus on safeguarding and protecting all children. Unlike the rest of the UK, Scotland has refrained from using the term 'safeguarding' to refer to this new policy direction; nevertheless the child protection net has been extended in a similar way.

Although there have been some legislative changes in England and Wales, most of the provisions of the Children Act 1989 still apply. The introduction of Children's Trusts and replacement of non-statutory Area Child Protection Committees with statutory Local Safeguarding Children Boards in the Children Act 2004 were designed to increase levels of accountability. Strengthening lines of accountability has been a major theme across the UK. In common with England and Wales, Northern Ireland also has plans to introduce new legislation to put child protection structures on a statutory footing. Reform in Scotland has contrasted with that in the rest of the UK because it has taken place within the confines of existing legislation. In contrast to England, Wales and Northern Ireland, Scotland has not gone down the statutory route or wholly embraced the 'safeguarding' agenda. While there are no plans to replace non-statutory Child Protection Committees in Scotland, their functions and membership have, however, been similarly extended and their lines of accountability and performance management arrangements similarly strengthened (Vincent, 2009).

CHAPTER 2

Every Child Matters: Change for Children programme in England

Nigel Parton, Phillip Noyes and Wendy Rose

Introduction

The focus of this chapter is to provide a review of the reform of child protection law and policy in England in recent years. In particular, we discuss the key elements of the *Every Child Matters: Change for Children* programme and the main changes it has introduced. We also consider the possible implications and impact of the tragic death of Baby Peter and how policy and practice may be changing as a result. We begin, however, with a brief discussion of the origins, aims and development of the contemporary child protection system in England.

The contemporary child protection system in England

Following the tragic death of Maria Colwell while under the supervision of local authority social workers and the subsequent public inquiry (Secretary of State for Social Services, 1974), a new system of child abuse management was inaugurated in England with the issue of a Department of Health and Social Security circular (Department of Health and Social Security, 1974). This was further refined in a series of government circulars throughout the decade (Department of Health and Social Security, 1976a; 1976b; 1978; 1980). The primary purpose of the system was to ensure that a range of key professionals were familiar with the signs of child abuse and that mechanisms were established so that information could be shared between them. Coordination between agencies and professionals was seen as key to improving practice, and the roles of paediatricians, GPs, health visitors and the police were seen as vital. However, it was social service departments that were constituted as the 'lead agency' and local authority social workers who were identified as the primary statutory professionals for coordinating the work and operating the system.

There were a number of key elements to the system. Area Review Committees, subsequently re-titled Area Child Protection Committees (ACPCs) (Department of Health and Social Security, 1988), were established in 1974 in all local authority areas as joint policy-making bodies in order to coordinate the work of the relevant agencies; develop inter-professional and multi-agency training; advise on the need for inquiries into cases which appeared to have gone wrong and from which lessons could be learned; and produce local detailed procedures to be followed where it was felt a child had been or might be at risk of abuse. In such situations a system of case conferences was established so that relevant professionals could share information about a particular child and family, make decisions on what to do and provide an ongoing mechanism for monitoring progress. Where it was felt a child protection plan was required the child would be placed on a Child Protection Register. The register could then be consulted by other professionals to establish whether the child was currently known.

However, increasingly in the 1980s a series of high profile scandals suggested that the child protection systems established were not working. Between the publication of the Maria Colwell Inquiry report in 1974 and 1985 there were 29 further inquiries into the deaths of children as a result of abuse (Corby et al., 1998). Some of these inquiries were set up locally by the authorities involved, others by central government (Department of Health and Social Security, 1982; Department of Health, 1991). There was considerable similarity in the findings. Most identified a lack of interdisciplinary communication, a lack of properly trained and experienced front-line workers, inadequate supervision and too little focus on the needs of the child as distinct from those of the parents. The overriding concern was the lack of coordination between different agencies. The intensity of political and media concern increased further in the mid-1980s with inquiries into three other child deaths in different London boroughs—Jasmine Beckford (London Borough of Brent, 1985), Tyra Henry (London Borough of Lambeth, 1987) and Kimberley Carlile (London Borough of Greenwich, 1987).

Until this point, all the inquiries had been concerned with the deaths of children at the hands of their parents or carers. Child welfare professionals were seen to have failed to protect the children and did too little too late. However, the Cleveland affair which broke in the summer of 1987 was very different. Over 100 children were kept in hospital against the wishes of their parents, on place of safety orders, on suspicion of sexual abuse (Secretary of State for Social Services, 1988; Parton, 1991).

The Children Act 1989, which continues to provide the primary legal framework in the field, aimed to provide a more integrated approach and attempted to introduce a new balance to law and practice. The central principles of the Act encouraged an approach based on negotiation with families and involving parents and children in agreed plans. The accompanying guidance and regulations encouraged professionals to work in partnership with parents and young people. The aim was to establish a new balance between supporting families with 'children in need' and the more forensically driven concerns of child protection, with a much greater emphasis on the former. A number of reports suggested, however, that local authorities were finding it difficult to implement the key principles and aims of the legislation in their agency policy and practice (Department of Health, 1994; Audit Commission, 1994).

However, the publication of *Child Protection: Messages from Research* (Department of Health, 1995), which summarised the key findings from a government-commissioned research programme, was to prove crucial in opening up a major debate about the future shape of child protection policy and practice in England (Parton, 1997). It demonstrated that only around one in seven of those referred to the statutory child welfare service as children at risk of abuse was ever subject to a child protection plan and placed on a Child Protection Register and fewer than one in 25 was ever removed from home as a result. The report argued that 'if we put to one side the severe cases' (p. 19), the most deleterious situations, in terms of longer-term outcomes for children, were those of emotional neglect and a parenting style that failed to compensate for the inevitable deficiencies that become manifest in the course of the twenty years or so it takes to bring up a child. Unfortunately, the research suggested, these were just the sort of situations where the forensically driven child protection system was least successful and many children and parents felt alienated and angry.

The key recommendation from the research was that policy and practice should be 're-focused' and should prioritise section 17 and Part III of the Children Act 1989, in terms of supporting families with children in need, rather than simply concentrating on investigating 'incidents' of abuse in a narrow forensically driven way. It was argued that policy and practice should be driven by an emphasis on partnership, participation, prevention and family support. The priority should be on helping parents and children in the community in a supportive way and should keep notions of policing and coercive interventions to a minimum where such action was required in the child's best interests. Subsequent government research, however, demonstrated that local authority social services departments, the primary statutory child welfare agency, continued to find it very difficult to 're-focus' their services in the ways suggested (Department of Health, 2001).

The other major development in the 1990s was the growth of concerns about ritual, organised and institutional abuse. These new concerns had a different relationship to the family; they were increasingly focused on extra-familial abuse rather than intra-familial abuse and, by the middle of the decade, were not just about residential homes but also day-care settings, sports clubs, youth clubs and the church. Concern about abuse in residential homes was initially prompted by revelations about the use of a particularly harsh system of punishment being operated in a number of children's homes in Staffordshire called 'Pindown' (Staffordshire County Council, 1991). The government responded by commissioning Sir William Utting to produce a 'special review of residential care' to improve the monitoring and control of residential care (Utting, 1991).

However, a series of allegations from all parts of the country quickly emerged about the sexual abuse of children in care, going back many years, which were the subject of police and social work investigations. It was the growing and widening concerns in North Wales and Merseyside that provided the increasingly complex backcloth to developments throughout the decade. While the final report was not published until 2000 (Waterhouse, 2000), many of the key issues had been identified in a review established by the government in 1996 and which was again chaired by Sir William Utting (1997). It quickly became known as the Safeguards Review and was to become a key document in helping to frame future policy and practice. While its focus was children living away from home, the concept of 'safeguarding' was in future to have a much wider significance. It argued that 'safeguard and promote are equal partners in an overall concept of welfare … and form the basis for ensuring physical and emotional health, good education and sound social development' (Utting, 1997, p. 15). These were to be important issues for the incoming New Labour government.

The New Labour government, social exclusion and the move to safeguarding

The New Labour government of Tony Blair was elected in May 1997. It quickly became apparent that it had a much broader view of the role of 'family support' than simply as a counterweight to a forensically focused approach to child protection evident in the 're-focusing' debate. Family support was seen as a major contributor to combat 'social exclusion' (Featherstone, 2004). New Labour came to power with a commitment to tackle problems which it saw as being particularly associated with social exclusion in certain neighbourhoods and sections of society, such as crime, anti-social behaviour and poor educational achievement. The role of parents was seen as crucial in overcoming such problems and it was therefore important not only to extend the role of the state, but to do so in a way that would support the role of parents in the most deprived communities and improve the prospects for poor children.

Social exclusion was defined almost exclusively in terms of people being excluded or marginalised from the labour market and a key priority was placed on improved educational attainment and getting people into paid work (Byrne, 2005; Levitas, 2005). Policies were also concerned with improving behaviour and social functioning and a variety of factors were seen as putting certain people, particularly the young, at risk of social exclusion, including poor parenting, not attending school, drug abuse, homelessness, unemployment and low income. The behaviour of children and young people was a particular concern and it was seen as very important that parents took their responsibilities seriously.

Policies focusing on children and young people were at the heart of the New Labour project to refashion the welfare state and tackle social exclusion, and a plethora of new policies were introduced and significant changes made to other long-established ones (Powell, 2008). While to some extent it could be argued the rationale for these policies was about ensuring that children would become responsible and economically active citizens, with the establishment of the Children's and Young People's Unit in the early days of the New Labour government there was some acknowledgement of the importance of childhood and the children's rights movement.

In this context child protection was seen as just one element in the ambitious attempts to 'modernise' and broaden the role of children's services in the context of trying to combat social exclusion. This shift in emphasis was made clear by a comparison of the official government guidance on *Working Together* published at the beginning and end of the 1990s. At the beginning of the decade the priority was clearly upon forensically investigating child abuse and the guidance was entitled *Working Together Under the Children Act 1989: A Guide to the Arrangements for Inter-agency Co-operation for the Protection of Children from Abuse* (Home Office *et al.*, 1991). As the subtitle states, the focus was clearly upon 'the protection of children from abuse' and the document was framed primarily in terms of when and how to carry out an investigation in terms of Section 47 of the Children Act 1989. The key decision was whether a case (referral/report) met the criteria for formal state intervention and whether the child was 'suffering or likely to suffer significant harm' (s.31(91)(9)).

By the end of the decade the guidance had been substantially rewritten and was entitled *Working Together to Safeguard Children: A Guide to Inter-agency Working to Safeguard and Promote the Welfare of Children* (Department of Health *et al.*, 1999). The words 'protection' and 'abuse' had been dropped from the title, which was now framed in terms to reflect the general duty placed on local authorities by Section 17(1) of the Children Act 1989 'to safeguard and promote the welfare of children in their area who are in need'. The guidance underlined the fact that local authority social services departments had much wider responsibilities than simply responding to concerns about child abuse and 'significant harm' and were explicitly located in the wider agenda for children's services being promulgated in the early years of the New Labour government. A whole variety of issues, apart from child abuse, were identified as 'sources of stress for children and families which might have a negative impact on a child's health, either directly, or because they affected the capacity of parents to respond to their child's needs' (Department of Health *et al.*, 1999, para. 2.19), including social exclusion, domestic violence, the mental illness of a parent or carer, and drug and alcohol misuse.

This shift in focus from the 'risk' of child abuse to 'children in need and their families' was even more evident in the language used to describe the way to approach 'assessments'. The publication of the 1999 edition of *Working Together* incorporated the new approach of more broadly based assessment of all children in need, including those where there were child protection concerns, in its guidance on handling individual cases (Chapter 5), published a few months later in full in the *Framework for the Assessment of Children in Need and their Families* (Department of Health,. 2000). Both documents were published by central government under Section 7 of the Local Authority Social Services Act 1970, which meant that they 'must be followed' by local authority social service departments unless there were exceptional circumstances that justified a variation. The assessment framework aimed to broaden the focus from investigation of child abuse and 'significant harm', when there were child protection concerns, to one which was concerned with the possible impairment to a child's development and early identification of additional needs. Both the safeguarding and the promotion of a child's welfare were seen as intimately connected aims for intervention, so that it was important that access to services was via a common assessment route. The critical task was to ascertain whether a child was 'in need' and how the child and their parents might be helped while, at the same time, acting quickly to secure the immediate safety of a child when required (Department of Health *et al.*, 1999, para. 5.23).

There was thus an explicit attempt to try and re-orientate policy and practice, where the emphasis was to be upon assessing and responding to a child's overall developmental needs in the context of their family and community. The concept of 'child protection' was superseded by the much broader notion of 'safeguarding and promoting the welfare of the child'. These ideas have been further developed in the most recent version of *Working Together*, published in 2006, and which was again called *Working Together to Safeguard Children: A Guide to Inter-Agency Working to Safeguard and Promote the Welfare of Children* (HM Government, 2006).

Effective measures to safeguard children were seen as those which also promoted their welfare, and should not be seen in isolation from the wider range of support and services provided to meet the needs of all children and families. The 2006 *Working Together* provided the first official definition of 'safeguarding' which, at the same time, stated how this related to the idea of 'child protection'. What becomes clear is that concerns to protect children from child abuse had not disappeared, but had been located in these wider concerns.

Safeguarding and promoting the welfare of children is defined for the purposes of this guidance as:

- protecting children from maltreatment;
- preventing impairment of children's health or development;
- ensuring that children are growing up in circumstances consistent with the provision of safe and effective care;

- undertaking that role so as to enable those children to have optimum life chances and to enter adulthood successfully (HM Government, 2006, para. 1.18).

Child protection was specifically related to attempts to assess and intervene in situations where children were suffering, or were likely to suffer, 'significant harm' and it was local authority statutory social workers who were to play the leading and central role in identifying where there were concerns about child maltreatment and deciding whether it might be necessary to consider taking urgent action to ensure that children were safe from harm (HM Government, 2006, para. 5.31).

The Every Child Matters: Change for Children programme

The 2006 *Working Together* guidance was published at a time of tremendous change in children's services in England, seen by many as the most significant change in the philosophy, organisation and delivery of children's services since 1948 (Hudson, 2005). The government had just launched its *Every Child Matters: Change for Children* (ECM) programme (HM Government, 2004), where the overriding vision was to bring about a 'shift to prevention whilst strengthening protection' (Department for Education and Skills, 2004, p. 3). The consultative Green Paper, *Every Child Matters* (Chief Secretary to the Treasury, 2003) was launched as the government's response to the very high profile public inquiry into the death of Victoria Climbié (Laming, 2003), although work on it had been underway for some time.

Victoria Adjo Climbié was born on the Ivory Coast in West Africa on 2 November 1991. Her aunt, Marie Therese Kouao, brought her to London in April 1999. In the following nine months the family was known to four different local authority social service departments, two hospitals, two police child protection teams and a family centre run by the National Society for the Prevention of Cruelty to Children. However, when she died on 25 February 2000, the Home Office pathologist found 128 separate injuries on her body as a result of being beaten by a range of sharp and blunt instruments. It was the worst case of deliberate harm to a child that he had ever seen. Marie Therese Kouao and her boyfriend, Carl Manning, were convicted of her murder in January 2001. The government immediately set up a public inquiry chaired by Lord Laming to investigate the involvement of the various public agencies in the case and to make recommendations for change to ensure that such a death could be avoided in the future. Lord Laming's report was published in January 2003 (Laming, 2003).

However, the changes introduced were much broader than being only concerned with trying to overcome the problems of identifying and responding to cases of child abuse appropriately. Following the policy direction already established by the New Labour government, the priority was to intervene at a much earlier stage in children's lives in order to prevent a range of problems in later life in relation to educational attainment, unemployment, crime and anti-social behaviour. The changes were only partially concerned with child abuse (Parton, 2006; 2008). It was to include all children, as it was felt that any child, at some point in their life, could be seen as vulnerable to some form of risk and therefore might require help. The idea was to identify problems at an early stage and before they become chronic.

While the Children Act 1989 was seen as continuing to provide the primary legislative framework for policy and practice, the government felt it needed strengthening in certain aspects. The key theme of the Children Act 2004 was to encourage partnership and sharpen accountability between a wide range of health, welfare and criminal justice agencies by:

- placing a new duty on agencies to cooperate among themselves and with other local partners to improve the well-being of children and young people so that all work to common outcomes (be healthy; stay safe; enjoy and achieve; make a positive contribution; achieve economic well-being) (Section 10);

- placing a duty on key agencies to safeguard children and promote their welfare (Section 11) through new statutory Local Safeguarding Children's Boards (Sections 13–16);

- the power to establish a national database or index (subsequently called ContactPoint), via secondary legislation and guidance, that would contain basic information about all children and young people to help professionals to work together to provide early support but where case details would not be included (Section 12);

- a requirement that all local authorities with children's services responsibilities appoint a Director of Children's Services and a Lead Council Member to be responsible for, as a minimum, education and children's social service functions (Sections 18 and 19); this would have the effect of bringing to an end unified and generic social services departments;

- enabling and encouraging local authorities, Primary Care Trusts and others to pool budgets into a Children's Trust, and share information better to support more joining up on the ground, with health, education and social care professionals working together based in the same location such as schools and children's centres (Section 10);

- creating an integrated inspection framework to assess how well services work together to improve outcomes for children (Sections 20-25); subsequently taken on by Ofsted (Office for Standards in Education);

- the requirement for local authorities to produce a single Children and Young People's Plan (Section 17 and Schedule 5);

- the creation of a Children's Commissioner (Sections 1–9).

The key aim was to increase integration in order to enhance prevention and early intervention.

The model informing the changes was derived from the public health approach to prevention and has been characterised as 'the paradigm of risk and protection-focussed prevention' (France and Utting, 2005), whereby the knowledge of risk factors derived from prospective longitudinal research is drawn upon to design particular early intervention programmes and to re-orientate mainstream services. What was particularly attractive to policy makers was that a range of generic personal and environmental 'risk factors' seemed to have been identified that might be able to pre-empt a number of social problems, including criminal behaviour, violence, drug abuse, educational failure, unsafe sexual behaviour, and poor mental health—all conceptualised as future negative outcomes. The Green Paper stated that 'we have a good idea what factors shape children's life chances. Research tells us that the risk of experiencing negative outcomes is concentrated in children with certain characteristics' (Chief Secretary to the Treasury, 2003, p. 17).

These included:

- low income and parental unemployment;
- homelessness;
- poor parenting;
- poor schooling;
- postnatal depression among mothers;
- low birth weight;
- substance misuse;
- individual characteristics, such as intelligence;
- community factors, such as living in a disadvantaged community.

The more risk factors children experienced, the more likely it was that they would experience 'negative outcomes' and it was 'poor parenting' that was seen to play the key role. Identifying the risk factors and intervening early provided the major strategy for overcoming the social exclusion of children and avoiding problems in later life.

At the centre of the changes was the ambition to improve the outcomes for all children and to narrow the gap between those who do well and those who do not. The outcomes are defined in terms of being healthy, staying safe, enjoying and achieving, making a positive contribution and achieving economic well-being. Together the five outcomes are seen as key to improving well-being in childhood and later life. Child protection and safeguarding and promoting children's welfare are just some elements which contribute to the 'staying safe' outcome, which also includes reducing childhood accidents and bullying, and feeling safe at home, at school and in the community more generally (HM Government, 2008).

To achieve the outcomes, the changes aimed to integrate health, social care, education and criminal justice and ensure that traditional, organisational and professional 'silos' were overcome, particularly in order to share information so that risks could be identified early. This required new organisational structures at both the central and local government levels and the use of a variety of new systems of information, communication and technology (ICT) in line with the ambitious e-government strategy for the public sector (Parton, 2008; Frost and Parton, 2009). As a result the rate of change since 2004 has been exceptional and the range and complexity of computer systems designed to screen and identify those in need of attention has grown considerably. This has posed particular challenges to agencies and front-line practitioners, as well as for the IT software companies in developing systems 'fit for purpose' (Frost and Parton, 2009; Peckover et al., 2009).

In the context of these considerable changes, effective measures to 'safeguard' children are seen primarily as those which also promote their welfare, and should not be seen in isolation from the wider range of support and services provided to meet the needs of all children and families. While protecting children from maltreatment is seen as important in order to prevent impairment to health and development, on its own it is not seen as sufficient to ensure that children are growing up in circumstances that ensure the provision of safe and effective care.

However, while all agencies and individuals should aim to proactively 'safeguard and promote the welfare of children', child protection is specifically related to attempts to assess and intervene in situations where children have suffered, or are likely to suffer, 'significant harm' and thereby 'protecting children from maltreatment'. It is 'significant harm' which provides the key 'threshold criterion' for compulsory intervention.

The current *Working Together* guidance is 260 pages in length (HM Government, 2006) and is made up of nine chapters (155 pages) of statutory guidance and four chapters (40 pages) of non-statutory practice guidance, together with six appendices (30 pages), plus an overall summary, introduction and definition of key terms.

In addition, every local authority and organisation which comes into contact with children has its own detailed procedures. Over the last 30 years child protection and child welfare work more generally have become increasingly proceduralised and subject to a plethora of complex government guidance. When professionals and organisations do not follow the guidance and procedures the consequences, particularly where things are seen to have gone wrong, can be considerable, including being sacked from the job, being removed from the respective professional register, strong criticisms from government inspectors, and media opprobrium.

Section II of the Children Act 2004 places a statutory duty on a wide range of agencies to ensure they have regard to 'safeguarding and promoting the welfare of children', i.e. wider than child protection. The organisations listed include all police, probation, prison and health bodies. The Children and Young Person's Act 2008 also places similar responsibilities upon schools and general practitioners.

For many years the prime strategy has been to encourage different professionals and organisations to 'work together' where there are child protection concerns and, more recently, where there are concerns about 'safeguarding and promoting the welfare of the child'. This was strengthened in 2006 with the establishment in all local authorities of statutory Local Safeguarding Children's Boards (LSCBs) for developing and coordinating safeguarding policies, practices, training and quality control in each local authority area. It includes the responsibility for the establishment of Serious Case Reviews, where a child has died or is seriously injured and abuse or neglect is known or suspected to be a factor; and Child Death Reviews where a child has died unexpectedly, irrespective of whether there are concerns about abuse and neglect.

The membership of LSCBs includes the senior managers from the local authority, the police, all hospitals and health organisations, probation, education, prisons and young offender organisations, together with representatives from non-government child welfare organisations operating in the area.

Working Together (HM Government, 2006) provides the statutory procedural framework and detailed guidance for responding to any 'concerns about a child's welfare', which is much broader than concerns about child maltreatment. The attempts to integrate child protection with a broader child welfare response, which have characterised the developments in England, are clearly evident, for the procedures for responding to concerns about child maltreatment are nested within the broader child welfare-orientated *Framework for the Assessment of Children in Need and their Families* (Rose, 2009).

Figure 2.1 provides a schematic summary of the nature and distribution of the work of local authority departments in England over a year and the key components of the different processes involved. What is demonstrated is that a major system has been established which aims to filter and categorise cases, but which is much broader than 'child protection'. From a starting point of 538,500 referrals to children's social care during the year ending 31 March 2008, just 34,000 were registered with a child protection plan (6% of the total referrals). A considerable amount of time, resources and professional judgement is invested in trying to manage such a complex and demanding series of decision-making processes and to ensure that children are protected and their needs met.

Furthermore, when we look at the national statistics on the distribution between the categories of abuse for cases registered with child protection plans since 1994, a very interesting trend emerges, as shown in Table 2.1. While the total has increased only slightly from 30,700 in 1994 to 34,100 in 2008, the distributions between the different categories of abuse have changed significantly:

- the absolute and percentage increase in registrations for neglect from 7,800 (25%) in 1994 to 15,300 (45%) in 2008;
- an increase in emotional abuse from 3,500 (11%) in 1994 to 8,600 (25%) in 2008;
- a decline in physical abuse from 11,400 (37%) in 1994 to 5,000 (15%) in 2008;
- a decline in sexual abuse registrations from 7,500 (24%) in 1994 to 2,300 (7%) in 2008.

As with all official statistics, of course, these professional responses do not

Figure 2.1 Children in each stage of the referral and assessment procedure, year ending 31 March 2008

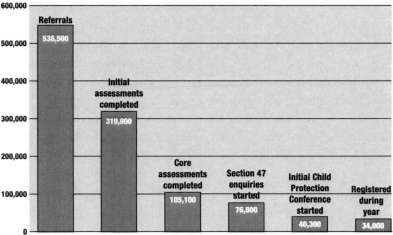

Source: Department for Children, Schools and Families (2008) *Referrals, Assessments and Children and Young People who are subject of a Child Protection Plan or on Child Protection Registers, England. Year ending 31 March 2008*

Table 2.1 Numbers and percentages of children with 'child protection plans' registered ending 31 March 1994 to 2008, by category of abuse, in England (alternate years)

Category of abuse	Numbers (%)							
	1994	1996	1998	2000	2002	2004	2006	2008
Neglect	7,800 (25%)	9,400 (31%)	11,600 (35%)	14,000 (41%)	10,800 (39%)	12,600 (41%)	13,700 (44%)	15,300 (45%)
Physical abuse	11,400 (37%)	10,700 (35%)	9,900 (30%)	8,700 (26%)	5,300 (19%)	5,700 (18%)	5,100 (16%)	5,000 (15%)
Sexual abuse	7,500 (24%)	6,200 (20%)	6,100 (18%)	5,600 (16%)	2,800 (10%)	2,800 (9%)	2,600 (8%)	2,300 (7%)
Emotional abuse	3,500 (11%)	4,000 (13%)	4,800 (15%)	5,500 (16%)	4,700 (17%)	5,600 (18%)	6,700 (21%)	8,600 (25%)
Mixed/not recommended by Working Together	500 (2%)	400 (1%)	700 (2%)	310 (1%)	4,100 (15%)	4,300 (14%)	3,300 (11%)	2,900 (8%)
TOTAL	30,700	30,700	33,100	34,110	27,700	31,000	31,400	34,100

Note: information compiled from government statistics

necessarily mirror children's actual experiences within families. However, putting these figures together, child protection plan registrations for neglect and emotional abuse accounted for 11,300 cases (37% of total) in 1994 but 23,900 cases (70%) in 2008, whereas child protection plans categorised as physical and sexual abuse accounted for 18,900 (62% of total) in 1994 but just 7,300 (21%) in 2008.

What we have suggested is that the period since 1997 has seen considerable change in policy and practice in England. More particularly, we have argued that, while far from straightforward, the general trend has been one which has attempted to broaden approaches to child protection in such a way that tries to prioritise prevention and early intervention and where the prime focus has become 'safeguarding and promoting the welfare of the child'. At the same time the changes have been driven by a strong 'performance-management' centrally driven framework, where the role of information communication technology has become central. Managers and practitioners, as a result, are spending an increasing amount of their time entering information into computers, and the administrative and bureaucratic demands of the work have increased inexorably together with the consequences for resources and practice.

The death of Baby Peter and the re-emergence of child protection

The radical changes introduced by the *Every Child Matters: Change for Children* programme were all planned to be in place during 2008. However, before the year was out the horrendous death of 17-month-old 'Baby P'—later known as (Baby) Peter Connelly—exploded into the media causing a huge political and public response.

On 11 November 2008, two men were convicted of causing or allowing the death of Baby Peter, one of whom was his stepfather. The baby's mother had already pleaded guilty to the charge. During the trial, the court heard that Baby Peter was used as a 'punch bag' but that his mother deceived and manipulated professionals with lies and on one occasion had smeared him with chocolate to hide his bruises. There had been over sixty contacts with the family from a variety of health and social care professionals and he was pronounced dead just 48 hours after a hospital doctor failed to identify that he had a broken spine. He was the subject of a child protection plan with Haringey Council and it was clear that serious discussions had taken place as to whether the council should be pursuing care proceedings in order to remove him from home.

The media response was immediate and very critical of the services, particularly the local authority and much of the attention was focused upon the role and public statements of the Director of Children's Services in Haringey, Sharon Shoesmith. Headlines such as 'Blunder Scandal of Baby Battered to Death' (*Daily Mirror*, 12 November), 'Blood on Their Hands' (*The Sun*, 12 November), '50 Injuries, 60 Visits—failures that led to the Death of Baby Peter' (*The Guardian*, 12 November) were quickly followed by the largest selling daily tabloid newspaper, *The Sun*, running a campaign to get the professionals involved in the case sacked from their jobs under the banner 'Beautiful Baby Peter: Campaign for Justice' (*The Sun*, 15 November). In this respect *The Sun*'s response mirrored earlier media campaigns directed at galvanising the government into action, as happened after the tragic death of James Bulger over a decade before (Franklin and Petley, 1996). Two weeks later the newspaper delivered a petition to the Prime Minister containing over 1.5 million signatures, claiming it was the largest and most successful campaign of its sort ever.

Ed Balls, the Secretary of State, responded to the furore by:

- ordering Ofsted, the Healthcare Commission and the police inspectorate to carry out an urgent Joint Area Review (JAR) of safeguarding in Haringey;

- ordering the preparation of a new and independent Serious Case Review following the publication of the original one on 12 November, which was deemed to be inadequate and insufficiently critical;

- appointing Lord Laming to carry out an urgent national review of child protection and to report in three months' time;

- establishing a 'Social Work Task Force' to identify any barriers that social workers face in doing their jobs effectively and to make recommendations for improvements and the long-term reform of social work and to report in the autumn.

On receipt of the JAR on 1 December, which he described as 'devastating', the Secretary of State announced he was using his powers under the Education Act 1996 to direct Haringey to remove Sharon Shoesmith from her post as Director of Children's Services. Later that month she was sacked by the council without compensation and with immediate effect. In April 2009 Haringey Council dismissed four other employees in relation to the Baby Peter case—the Head of Children in Need and Safeguarding Services, the Deputy Director of Children's Services, the Team Manager, and the allocated Social Worker.

Very quickly reports were surfacing that it was becoming extremely difficult to recruit and retain staff nationally to work in children's social care, particularly qualified social workers, and morale was said to be at an all-time low (Local Government Association, 2009). The case was clearly having wide scale reverberations. A number of influential commentators, including the Children, Schools and Families Commons Committee (2009), began to argue that the threshold for admitting children into state care was too high. Not only should Baby Peter have been admitted to care some months prior to his death but the situation he was in was not unusual. Similarly CAFCASS (2009), the Children and Family Court Advisory and Support Service, produced figures which demonstrated that there were nearly 50% more care applications in the second half of 2008–9 compared to the first half of the year, demand for care cases was 39% higher in March 2009 compared to March 2008, and that the demand for care continued to remain at an unprecedentedly high level for the first quarter of 2009–10 with June 2009 having the highest demand for care ever recorded for a single month.

In this context it is worth considering why the case had such a strong and prolonged reaction. First, this was clearly a horrific case which was always likely to invoke an angry response to the failures of the agencies involved. Second, Baby Peter died in Haringey, one of the local authorities which was heavily implicated and criticised in the Public Inquiry into the death of Victoria Climbié. As a number of commentators said, you would assume that of all the local authorities in the country Haringey would have put its house in order after the original *Laming Report* (2003). Third, Baby Peter was the subject of a child protection plan and was on the Haringey Child Protection Register—unlike Victoria Climbié who was only ever responded to as a 'family support' case. There were very many concerns expressed by a range of professionals on the grounds that this was clearly a very high risk case that had never been managed as such. Fourth, the government had claimed that it had introduced its *Every Child Matters: Change for Children* programme as a response to the *Laming Inquiry Report* into the death of Victoria Climbié to ensure that such a failure must never happen again.

The case of Baby Peter thus had the potential at best to raise questions and at worst undermine the major reform programme of the previous four years—just at the time when it was meant to be coming to fruition. In particular, many of the systems introduced seemed 'not fit for purpose'. The new information communication technologies, particularly those supporting the Integrated Children's System, came in for major criticism and were to be reviewed by the Social Work Task Force. But, in addition, the new inspection frameworks introduced by Ofsted did not seem to identify the problems in Haringey, and the independence and rigour of the Local Safeguarding Children's Boards seemed quite inadequate. In a political context where the Conservative opposition was looking to use any opportunity to criticise the government at a particularly difficult time, politically and economically, the government was keen to be seen as acting firmly and authoritatively. In fact a remarkable political consensus was established in support for 'child protection' and social workers. A significant political divide was evident only in relation to the existence and future of the information-sharing system ContactPoint, and whether Serious Case Reviews should be published in summary or in full.

Finally, the role of the media is important. *Panorama*, the long-standing BBC investigative documentary programme, had been conducting detailed background research on the Baby Peter case for some months earlier in 2008 with a view to having a major programme on it once the court case had been finalised. In the event, the programme was televised in its regular Monday night slot, six days after the story had broken. However, it is clear the research it had carried out very much informed the extensive and detailed coverage given to the case across the BBC news and comment programmes.

The high profile campaign run by *The Sun* newspaper mobilised public opinion, with around 1.5 million signing up to its 'Justice for Baby Peter' campaign that called for Haringey social workers and managers in the case to be sacked. In addition a number of Facebook groups, comprising over 1.6 million members, were set up in memory of Baby Peter and seeking justice for his killers. This weight of expressed opinion put major pressure on Ed Balls to be seen to be acting and to be taking control of the situation.

Conclusion

It is still early days to assess the likely longer-term impact of the Baby Peter case on the *Every Child Matters: Change for Children* programme. Apart from engendering a sense of high anxiety and vigilance among children's services managers and practitioners, it is possible to identify two significant developments: we seem to have rediscovered both 'child protection' and 'professional social work'.

It is notable that the report produced by Lord Laming in March 2009 was entitled *The Protection of Children in England: A Progress Report* and both this and the government's response (HM Government, 2009) were very much framed in terms of child protection. Whereas previously policy and practice was framed in terms of 'safeguarding and promoting the welfare of the child', it now seemed that concerns about child protection had, again, moved centre stage. The detail of how policy and practice may change as a result of this will become clearer with the rewriting of *Working Together*, which is scheduled for completion in early 2010.

And, in addition to rediscovering child protection, we also seem to have rediscovered professional social work. It is one of the great ironies that the area of practice where social work has been so heavily criticised for many years, child protection, is an area where it is seen as having the key role to play and the failures in the Baby Peter case seem to have reinforced that even further. The work of the Social Work Task Force is clearly central in this regard. However, the government has made it clear that the improvement in child protection which is required is crucially dependent on the rejuvenation of a well trained, respected and highly professionalised social work service. It is as if it is now recognised that child protection is complex, skilled and very demanding work. While improving systems and interagency communication is important, improving the service is vitally dependent on supporting and investing in a professional social work workforce. These are interesting developments.

CHAPTER 3

Children and young people: rights to action in Wales

Jonathan Corbett, Wendy Rose

Introduction

The aim of this chapter is to outline the policy direction being taken by the Welsh Assembly Government since devolution to safeguarding children and young people in Wales. Until devolution, England and Wales shared the same legislation and policy regarding safeguarding and child protection. Variations in guidance and in implementation reflected differences in circumstances but were not significant. There are now indications of a more marked divergence in policy and in implementation.

A brief resumé of the landscape in Wales

Devolution in Wales was a policy ambition achieved by the general election result in 1997 and the Government of Wales Act 1998 soon followed. Since then devolution has been an evolving process and change is continuing even now. As it evolves, there are signs of increasing divergence between England and Wales. This can be said to be 'a good thing', but it also poses a number of challenges, which are explored in this chapter in the context of safeguarding reform. Delivery of services through integrated social services remains the cornerstone of the Welsh approach, particularly in meeting the needs of vulnerable people. In Wales 'social services' is still the correct term, which marks the first point of divergence with England where 'children's social care' and 'adult social care' reflect major organisational and structural change in the last decade.

Wales currently has a population of just over 3 million people. There are twenty-two unitary local authorities whose population size varies between about 60,000 in the smallest and 300,000 in the largest. Local authorities have until recently been co-terminus with twenty-two Local Health Boards and a smaller number of National Health Service Trusts. However, following a significant period of consultation, the Minister for Health and Social Services announced that from October 2009 there would be major NHS reform in Wales (Welsh Assembly Government, 2009a). The Local Health Boards and Trusts have been swept away and replaced by seven new Local Health Boards, providing most mainstream health care across Wales. As Pithouse (forthcoming) has observed, NHS reform in Wales 'has formally ended any pretence of an internal market'. This reorganisation inevitably has implications for local authorities and social services, not least in the short term because, as always happens in any major public service reorganisation, during the transition the health service is beginning to focus in on itself.

Two pieces of legislation set up the Welsh Assembly Government and the National Assembly for Wales. The Government of Wales Act 1998 established the National Assembly as a single corporate body with secondary legislative powers and sixty assembly members. The new arrangements subsequently provided in the Government of Wales Act 2006 created a legal separation between the National Assembly, which is the legislature, and the Welsh Assembly Government, the executive. This separation between legislature and executive took effect in May 2007, following the last Assembly Government elections. Wales now has its third government since devolution which is a coalition between Labour and Plaid Cymru. It has a programme of work to which the two parties have committed themselves, under the title *One Wales* (Labour and Plaid Cymru Groups, 2007). This sets the strategic framework and objectives for four years because, as in Scotland and Northern Ireland, governments are elected for four-year periods.

The legislative powers given to the Assembly in the Government of Wales Act 2006, Schedule 5, represented a major step forward. The Assembly is now able to seek *legislative competence* from the UK Parliament, effectively to make its own primary legislation. These are called Assembly Measures and it is not a straightforward process to get to the point where an Assembly Measure can be made. This can be done in one of three ways: by seeking agreement from the UK Parliament to make a new category of legislation called a Measure, or by seeking legislative competence through clauses in Parliamentary Bills, or through a new order in council procedure provided for in the Government of Wales Act 2006.

Although a relatively new process in Wales, a number of areas of legislative competence have been secured, most notably for children by means of a Vulnerable Children Measure. These powers were devolved to the National Assembly in December 2008. This means that in terms of health, social services and education, where the Assembly has that competence, it can effectively now make its own legislation. Work has been underway to enable a consolidation Measure to be made that would bring together all the different parts of legislation affecting children into one new Measure. In relation to vulnerable children and child poverty the Assembly Government has introduced a Measure, the Children and Families (Wales) Measure 2009, that among other provisions is taking forward a distinct agenda to eradicate poverty and provide greater support to children living in families with complex needs, where family members have difficulties with drug misuse, domestic violence, abusive behaviour or mental disorder.

In 2007, the Assembly Government published *Fulfilled Lives, Supportive Communities* (Welsh Assembly Government, 2007b), aimed at improving social services in Wales over a ten-year period from 2008 to 2018. It describes how modernised social services will contribute to a better Wales and to improving the lives of its citizens. It was the product of a widespread consultation process and it was the Assembly Government's intention to modernise social services in order to provide more accessible personal care for people, ensuring they are supported earlier and helped to retain their independence for longer. *Fulfilled Lives, Supportive Communities* was developed to complement the health service strategy *Designed for Life* (Welsh Assembly Government, 2007a). *Fulfilled Lives, Supportive Communities* was addressed primarily to local authorities, which have responsibility for planning and commissioning social services for vulnerable people in a range of partnerships. It requires active engagement from many more people— service users, their carers, families and service providers as well as the statutory and third sectors—and the workforce must be involved and listened to if the changes and improvements encapsulated in these two strategies are to be achieved.

Similarly, in 2006, the Assembly Government published *Making the Connections – Delivering Beyond Boundaries* (Welsh Assembly Government, 2006b). This followed a review of local public service delivery in Wales, chaired by Sir Jeremy Beecham (Welsh Assembly Government, 2006a). This provides an overall framework for public service delivery in the context of Wales, which has been developed further in a number of specific policy statements and consultations. The government is also introducing a new local government Measure which will include a framework for the future of regulation, audit and inspection. There is a wide-ranging programme of reform to boost the capacity and transform the culture and performance of public services in Wales over the next five years. The aim is that public service organisations will become more responsive to citizens and communities, more integrated in the way they deliver services to people, more efficient in the way they are managed, and more effective in leading and supporting the workforce through the challenges.

This provides a broad overview of the framework within which the reform programme for improving the lives of children and young people is developing in Wales. Underpinning this programme is, as Sharon Vincent identifies in her overview in Chapter 1, the importance attached in Wales to a rights-based approach, founded on the UN Convention on the Rights of the Child, and to the seven core aims that provide the overall framework for work in relation to children and children's services in Wales (Welsh Assembly Government, 2004).

The Children Act 2004 and current safeguarding reforms

The Children Act 2004 is a significant starting point with regard to issues of safeguarding and the approach being taken in Wales. As has been outlined in the Chapter 2, the Act followed the Victoria Climbié Inquiry (Laming, 2003). In Wales, immediately after the Inquiry (and this did not happen in any of the other countries of the UK), a full audit and verification of compliance with all the recommendations in Lord Laming's report was carried out in each of the twenty-two local authorities. Interestingly, five years later, before the death of Baby P (Peter Connelly) came under the media spotlight, consideration was being given by officials to undertaking a further audit to assess the progress that had been made. When the Joint Area Review report about the death of Baby Peter hit the headlines, what had been thought might be required, rapidly and within a matter of hours, became a pressing reality. However, the environment in Wales for this action was quite different from that in England. Officials had worked closely with Ministers throughout to try and take a very measured approach, because as Professor Pithouse said at the UK seminar (January 2009), 'Baby Peter could happen anywhere, at any time'. It is important to recognise that there had been a steady programme of work over the past five to ten years aimed at addressing fundamental problems in the safeguarding system that had been identified earlier through social services audits and inspections. There was no wish at government level to see that work unravelling overnight, something that could easily have happened in a higher octane political or media environment.

Ministers in Wales have, therefore, taken a measured approach. As a result, during 2009 the Care and Social Services Inspectorate Wales (CSSIW) undertook an audit of all local authorities' safeguarding arrangements (Care and Social Services Inspectorate Wales, 2009c). Teams of inspectors, between March and May 2009, visited all twenty-two authorities. A team of two or three inspectors spent two or three days in each authority, looking at a range of areas of activity. All local authorities had had to complete a self-audit exercise, the reports of which were returned for analysis. Basically the Inspectorate had been looking at the evidence to verify whether what local authorities were saying was justified.

Local Safeguarding Children Boards have also been the subject of reviews and similarly during 2009 have had to assess their effectiveness and report on this to the Inspectorate. Furthermore, there has been a major programme of work in train to examine the effectiveness of Serious Case Reviews. Interestingly, there was a meeting in Wales in 2006 where the intention to review the Serious Case Review process was first set out because of increasing concerns that the current arrangements were not working as intended. However, experience of government shows that there is often a right moment to take forward particular pieces of work, and that moment in respect of Serious Case Reviews came at the end of 2008, following the revision of *Safeguarding Children: Working Together under the Children Act 2004* (Welsh Assembly Government, 2006c) and the Baby Peter case.

What has been undertaken in Wales is a programme of work around safeguarding that culminated in a series of reports which were presented to Ministers and published in the autumn of 2009 (Care and Social Services Inspectorate Wales, 2009c; 2009b). Ministers have taken account of what has been found in Wales, and considered these findings in the context of *Lord Laming's Progress Report* (Laming, 2009) and the work in England of the National Safeguarding Delivery Unit (National Safeguarding Delivery Unit, 2009) and the Social Work Task Force. The arrangements and next steps needed to strengthen the safeguarding and protection of children in Wales were announced to the Welsh Assembly on 21 October 2009. This carefully prepared approach prevented Wales from being bounced into action or a new direction simply because of the pressure of what was happening elsewhere in the UK. The Children Act 2004 has been important in setting the framework in Wales for the major programme of safeguarding improvement and reform that is underway and will be carried forward over the next several years.

The role of social services

Returning to the role of social services, as already stated there is a ten-year strategy in place for transforming social services. What has been recognised is that social services are heavily interdependent services both internally and in their external relationships. Effective social services depend on engaging with a wide variety of partnerships with other council services and external agencies. They are delivered through a substantial mixed market of providers and it is critical that social services maintain a coherence that ensures a seamless and safe service for users, particularly in relation to the safety and welfare of children and their families. Parents receive assistance from adult services to support them in parenting their children as effectively as possible. Service users with continuing care needs have transitions at different stages in their lives that require sensitive management in order to optimise their independence and well-being and to realise their potential and opportunities. Ensuring an adequate and skilled workforce that is planned and developed in an integrated way is critical so that the strengths and opportunities interconnected services provide are maximised. These are important elements of integrated social services that are delivered under the unified leadership of the Director of Social Services.

The Children Act 2004 gave rise to a number of key developments. Section 25 of the Act made provision for statutory children and young people's partnerships, in which local authorities have a duty to take a lead in driving forward cooperation, and put in place arrangements to improve the well-being of children and young people. Section 26 provides for a statutory children's plan in relation to children and relevant young persons. The children and young people's partnership is responsible for the development and delivery of a single children's plan. This is the key statement of planning intent embracing the whole range of services for children across local government and other agencies. It provides strategic vision, stating the agreed priorities and targets, and provides a more robust basis for joint commissioning of services.

Wales has just come to the end of the first round of planning, which has resulted in three-year strategic plans being produced. It is an evolving process and Wales is still at the stage of seeing how effectively these partnerships are able to work together in developing and delivering their plans. It is fair to say, before the single children and young people's plan was introduced, officials in government tried to count the number of different plans that different partnerships and organisations were required to produce and there was some incredulity about how those involved in partnerships ever had time to do any work other than produce plans. The plans were then sent to the Assembly Government where they were probably used as very effective insulation of the mezzanine floor in Cathays Park. So there has been a major change, which it is hoped will become a significant driver for ensuring agencies look much more carefully at how they work together and how they plan strategically for the delivery of services for children.

The significance of a lead director for children and young people's services

The Children Act 2004 also required local authorities to identify a lead director for children and young people's services and a lead member, together with their equivalents in NHS bodies. Wales, unlike England, decided to retain social services departments. The new requirements of the legislation resulted for a time in a degree of confusion in Wales about the role of the lead director, because in England new children's services departments were being set up and directors of children's services being appointed. The role in Wales is essentially to take the lead in promoting and coordinating planning for children and young people, no more and no less. They do not carry operational responsibility for the delivery of all children's services as in England. In reality it is either the director of education or the director of social services in Wales who is fulfilling the lead director role for coordinating multi-agency planning for children and young people.

Guidance was produced on the lead director role within the children and young people's partnerships, and the role of the director of the social services was further elaborated in a number of chief inspectors' annual reports. Building on this, statutory guidance laid out the role and accountabilities of the director of social services (National Assembly for Wales, 2006, No. 56) as follows:

- providing clear professional leadership across social services;

- having direct access to and advising the chief executive and councillors on social services matters and on directions and actions to be taken for fulfilling its social services responsibilities;
- ensuring strong performance management arrangements are in place across social services;
- reporting at a corporate level and to members on the authority's performance in respect of these;
- ensuring the authority has proper safeguards to protect vulnerable children and young people, adults and older people;
- reporting at a corporate level to members on their effectiveness;
- fulfilling overall responsibility for the social services workforce planning and training and professional development;
- ensuring there are adequate arrangements in place for social services to work effectively with others both inside and outside the authority in fulfilling its social services functions;
- contributing to the achievement of wider policy objectives.

Although government hoped that this guidance was clear, it transpired that there were twenty-two different ways of interpreting the role in Wales.

In the last five years, four authorities have been identified within Wales where there were serious concerns about children's social services. As a result, the serious concern protocol agreed between the Assembly Government and the Welsh Local Government Association (National Assembly for Wales, 2003) has been invoked by the Chief Inspector and has enabled him to require improvements in these local authorities. Furthermore, as a result of the experience of those authorities where social services were in difficulties, the conclusion was reached that, despite the existing guidance on the role of the director, local authorities still were not clear about what it really meant in practice. In some authorities, the director of social services was in reality little more than a name plate on a door.

It was decided, therefore, to produce further guidance setting out in far more detail what was entailed in the role and responsibilities of the director of social services in Wales (Welsh Assembly Government, 2009b). Some of the sections in the guidance have particular significance for safeguarding improvement and reform. It had become evident that there was some continuing confusion in relation to safeguarding about issues of independence, accountability and responsibility. The guidance sets out to clarify these issues once and for all. First, the guidance emphasises that the director of social services must have a sufficient level of seniority, with direct access to the head of paid service (i.e. the Chief Executive) and to councillors. This level of seniority is seen as essential for the effective discharge of the director's responsibilities for the authority's social services functions, for the delivery of those accountabilities, for performance and improvement, and for effective working relationships with other officers and organisations. The Welsh Assembly Government is absolutely clear that it is not its role to tell local authorities how to structure themselves—that is a matter for them to determine according to their local circumstances—but they must have in place a director of social services who fulfils these particular functions at the appropriate senior level. Importantly, the director reports directly to the head of paid service and must be a member of the top management team. This is a very important statement as there were some authorities where the director was operating at a third tier level of management within the authority, where they could neither discharge their responsibilities nor do their job effectively.

Second, with respect to child and adult safeguarding arrangements and reporting, the director of social services will:

- oversee and report to members on the operation, monitoring and improvement of child and adult protection safeguarding systems;
- ensure the effective operation of local safeguarding children's board and adult protection committees;
- ensure the application of emerging evidence to inform social services and interagency work on earlier intervention and prevention;
- raise the profile, support the policy and ensure adherence to practice to the extant guidance on adult protection;
- take steps to ensure all staff in children's and adults' social services and in other agencies understand and operate high standards of risk recognition and safeguarding practice, and to ensure thorough training, professional supervision and other opportunities for learning and reflection;
- ensure that staff involved in safeguarding work are properly supported, and promote greater public awareness of child and adult protection matters.

And finally, and most importantly, the guidance emphasises that, while all staff have responsibility to safeguard and promote the welfare of children, the director of social services remains the senior officer within the council, with final and indivisible accountability for this. In relation to vulnerable adults, the statutory basis for responsibility is less clear-cut and firm than for safeguarding children; however, the responsibility for taking the lead in ensuring effective local procedures rests with social services for which the director is accountable. This amounts to a very strong and important framework and message for local authorities.

As part of their public accountability, directors of social services have been given the responsibility for making an annual report to their local authority on the delivery and performance of their services, as well as outlining the plans for the improvement of social services functions.

The guidance lays out recommended competencies for the appointment of the director of social services. The first and critically important expect-ation is that they should have substantial experience at senior management level in social services or social care. The subsequent detailed list of expect-ations addresses some of the outstanding issues about where responsibility and accountability rest.

Local Safeguarding Children Boards

The Children Act 2004 not only set up the children and young people's partnerships and the requirement to produce a children and young people's plan, it also established the Local Safeguarding Children Boards (LSCBs) which, as has been stated in the previous chapter, replaced the former Area Child Protection Committees (ACPCs) in England and Wales, the differ-ence being that it put them on a statutory basis, broadened their remit and also identified who the statutory members were of the LSCB. They are the local authority, police, probation, youth offending, health—both in terms of the Local Health Boards and Trusts—and governors of any secure estab-lishments or prisons.

The LSCB functions were to coordinate what was being done by each body represented on the LSCB for the purposes of safeguarding and promoting the welfare of children in the area and to ensure the effectiveness of what was done. The focus of the LSCB remains the protection of children from abuse and neglect. The implications of this are that policies and practice should therefore be primarily targeted at those children who are suffering, or are at risk of suffering, significant harm. And, interestingly, the issues with which LSCBs in Wales have struggled are: what does safeguarding mean?; what are the boundaries?; how far do we go?; how wide does this responsibility go?;

and, if we broaden the boundaries, do we actually lose our focus on child protection?

Wales has, as mentioned in Sharon Vincent's overview in Chapter 1, *All Wales Child Protection Procedures*. They are not statutory procedures. They are not issued by the Welsh Assembly Government; the Welsh Assembly Government position is set out in the guidance *Safeguarding Children: Working Together under the Children Act 2004* (Welsh Assembly Government, 2006c). The *All Wales Child Protection Procedures* are the result of the former ACPCs, now the LSCBs, taking the lead across Wales and commissioning one set of procedures to which all have signed up and to which they all work, not on a statutory but on a voluntary basis. This approach has been continued by the LSCBs and is a model that has since been adopted in other parts of the UK, including London. It has been a major step forward in achieving a greater consistency of approach and indicative of what can be done differently in a country with a smaller number of local authorities working in a different relationship with the national government. This has been described as 'a model of public service provision for Wales that is publicly provided and delivered through a predominantly cooperative rather than competitive framework' (Pithouse, forthcoming).

Conclusions: challenges and the way ahead

Local Safeguarding Children Boards

Finally, some brief comments on the challenges and the way forward. It has been clear that Local Safeguarding Children Boards are still not mature and not working as effectively as they could. As a result, the Care and Social Services Inspectorate Wales commissioned the late Tony Morrison and Jan Howarth in 2008 to work with them and to develop a self audit and improvement tool for all Safeguarding Children Boards, launched in the spring of 2009. The development of this tool has been received very positively by LSCBs. It is being benchmarked, which means that, in coming years as LSCBs improve, the bar can be raised. The review by the Care and Social Services Inspectorate Wales (Care and Social Services Inspectorate Wales, 2009c) confirmed that LSCBs across Wales were at very different stages of their development and many were not yet effectively discharging their functions, not least because of problems of leadership, inadequate resourcing and business support arrangements, and the impact of size on capacity in some smaller authorities. In 2010 a joint inspection of Local

Safeguarding Children Boards is planned involving the Care and Social Services Inspectorate of Wales, the Wales Audit Office, Estyn (the Wales Education Inspectorate), the Health Inspectorate Wales and HMI Probation and HMI Constabulary, and the improvement programme will continue.

Workforce development

The workforce is clearly a huge challenge. Policies and procedures may be in place, but without staff services cannot be delivered and improvements in safeguarding children cannot be achieved. There has been a major workforce strategy in place for a number of years and social services are in a much better position now than five or six years ago. Wales could be more or less self-sufficient in social workers in the near future. Having made great progress in growing its own workforce, the next challenge is how to retain staff and ensure sustained professional development.

There is another stream of work underway examining the children's social work professional career pathway. What should such a career pathway look like? Once a social worker has qualified, does that mean he or she should be able to go into a post in an authority and be expected to do everything? Or should there be a stage-by-stage process that determines the level of work to which newly qualified social workers can progress according to an assessment of their experience, supervision and continuing professional development? These are issues being addressed more broadly across the children's workforce as a whole.

Working in partnership

A further challenge is that of partnership: partnership working is very easy to preach, but very difficult to practice (reinforced in the literature by researchers and other commentators, such as Hudson *et al.*, 1999; Horwath, 2009; Sidebotham and Weeks, 2010). It will not be any easier in the environment of diminishing public resources. The danger is that such a difficult context will undermine partnership working and push staff in the opposite direction, because inevitably their first concern will be to protect their own services, rather than embracing the complex task of working in partnership. It is recognised that there will have to be concerted national and local leadership working at trying to help staff—managers and practitioners—not to narrow their focus and become more inward-looking. Worrying public expenditure forecasts are going to present some significant challenges as well as opportunities over the next few years—how broadly safeguarding is defined is one such challenge, as already mentioned.

Local commitment and leadership

In terms of local authorities, it is demonstrated time and time again that there has to be strong political and corporate leadership, underpinned by strong professional leadership and clear accountability, if robust, effective and safe services are to be delivered. There is no doubt about that. If these services are not aligned and in place, it is only a matter time before something will go wrong.

Working positively with the media

Reference is made to the media in other chapters and to the challenges of operating in a twenty-first century public environment. Experience shows that the media response very much depends on the circumstances. There have been examples of difficult Serious Case Reviews that have not been picked up by the media and of others that have. It seems to depend on the other news of that day. What is clear is that the media in Wales are not interested in good news stories. In 2008 one Welsh authority had a very good joint review. It contacted the local newspaper and said to them 'we have had this very good joint review – would you like to publicise it?' The newspaper was not interested. The media reasoned that 'this is actually what you should be doing, it is your job to deliver a good service' and therefore there was no story.

The Chief Inspector's Annual Report for Social Services in Wales was published at the beginning of 2009 (Care and Social Services Inspectorate Wales, 2009a). The overall message contained within the report was: 'children's services are improving—there is lots of work to be done, but things are improving'. The media were all lined up for the publication of the report. Based on previous experience, it was thought they would want to talk to the Chief Inspector. However, while Swansea Sound and Red Dragon radio stations were interested for very specific local reasons, ITV took one look at the report and cancelled the interview. They simply were no longer interested. This was too much of a good news story. There is an important message here about how public service agencies, nationally and locally, work with the media and how the messages are better managed.

The role of the Inspectorates

In Wales it is for the Welsh Assembly Government to set a clear strategic direction and framework, which is then put into operation at a local level. What then are the roles of the inspectorates? The role of the Care and Social Services Inspectorate Wales is threefold: to encourage improvement of social care and social services through inspection; to promote improvement through the provision of expert, professional advice to ministers and policy makers; and to provide public assurance. However, the other side of the coin to supporting improvement is also to challenge core practice. It has to be recognised that safeguarding is complex work. It requires people to work together effectively and to keep the child at the centre of all their activity. And that, even in the best of circumstances, remains the greatest challenge.

CHAPTER 4

Our children and young people— our shared responsibility: the reform implementation process in child protection services in Northern Ireland

John Devaney, Fionnuala McAndrew, Tony Rodgers

Introduction

Northern Ireland is the smallest and youngest part of the United Kingdom. And yet, over the past forty years, Northern Ireland has experienced greater social and political changes than any other part of the United Kingdom. In spite of this, the issue of child protection has remained at the forefront of public and professional concerns. In this chapter the authors will outline how the system for protecting children from abuse and neglect has evolved over recent years in Northern Ireland. In particular we will discuss some of the recent major events that have shaped the child protection landscape and the reforms that have been developed and implemented following the publication in 2006 of a major review into the operation of the child protection system.

The origins of the contemporary child protection system in Northern Ireland

Northern Ireland contains a population of 1.8 million people, with the largest proportion of children (25%) in the four countries making up the United Kingdom (Office for National Statistics, 2009).

The signing of the Anglo-Irish Treaty in 1921 separated the island of Ireland into two distinct legal jurisdictions, one part of which remained within the United Kingdom. Between 1921 and 1972 affairs in Northern Ireland were administered by the local government. The Parliament of Northern Ireland was bicameral, consisting of a lower chamber (the House of Commons) and an indirectly elected upper chamber (the Senate). The Sovereign was represented by the Governor, who granted Royal Assent to Acts of Parliament in Northern Ireland, with executive power resting with the Prime Minister, the leader of the largest party in the Northern Ireland House of Commons.

Child welfare services in Northern Ireland were influenced, as in other parts of the United Kingdom, by the impact of both world wars. The government produced a White Paper that mirrored the sentiment of the 1946 *Report of the Care of Children Committee* (the Curtis Report) in England and Wales, bringing greater recognition to the needs of vulnerable children and the need for the state to provide better protection to particular children. The Children and Young Person's Act 1950 vested responsibility for children's welfare services in eight newly established public bodies, setting up 'welfare committees' to oversee the discharge of statutory responsibilities towards vulnerable children. These committees were the forerunner of the systems currently in place.

The welfare committees were charged with replacing the Poor Law provisions and workhouses with 'a new regime and culture of care and commitment to the well-being of vulnerable children' (Department of Health, Social Services and Public Safety, 2003a, p. 10). This involved the establishment of children's homes and a fostering service, and an increasing focus on the training needs of staff.

The Report of the Committee on Children and Young People 1960 (the Ingleby Report) highlighted the need for powers to combat child neglect, ill-treatment and juvenile offending. As Hendrick (2003) notes, the committee, while preoccupied with juvenile delinquency, linked depravation clearly with deprivation. The report recommended that local authorities should be given the general duty to engage in preventative work with children and their families and to provide therapeutic services. This focus on prevention was enshrined in the Children and Young Person's Act (Northern Ireland) 1968, with local welfare committees empowered to provide material assistance as a means of preventing children coming into care. This chimed with the main conclusions of *The Report of the Committee on Local Authority and Allied Personal Social Services 1968* (the Seebohm Report) that promoted the concept of generic community-based social services departments.

In the late 1960s the modern 'troubles' began, with clashes between civil rights activists and the police leading to civil unrest and increasing levels of paramilitary violence. This resulted in the Westminster government removing control of security from the government of Northern Ireland in 1972 and appointing a Secretary of State for the province. The Stormont government resigned en masse in protest at this perceived assault on their powers. The British Prime Minister responded by immediately introducing what would become known as 'direct rule'—the governance of Northern Ireland from Westminster.

The Westminster government acted swiftly in addressing a number of the complaints raised during the period of civil unrest. One of the major criticisms of local government was that it had been the cause of many of the grievances of civil rights protestors, fuelled by religious and political discrimination, for example over the allocation of social housing. As the government in London had no intention of directly empowering the local communities that were engaged in both inter-communal and anti-state violence, it established a number of democratically unaccountable, but well resourced, public service agencies, including integrated health and social services organisations (Pinkerton and Campbell, 2002). This created four Health and Social Services Boards with responsibility for the delivery of community and hospital-based health services. These contained new generic social services departments with responsibilities similar to local authorities in Great Britain.

Due to the nature of direct rule, child care policy in Northern Ireland became increasingly influenced by events and developments in Great Britain, and England in particular. The tragic death of Maria Colwell and the subsequent public inquiry (Secretary of State for Social Services, 1974) raised public awareness of the abuse and neglect of children, and political concern for robust and appropriate professional responses. This resulted in the establishment of many of the initial structures and processes of the current child protection system in both England and Northern Ireland (Kirton, 2008).

However, policy and practice in Northern Ireland were also influenced by local factors. In 1976 a committee of inquiry was established to review the entire corpus of child care provision in Northern Ireland as concerns existed about the rise in juvenile delinquency and the potential involvement of children in civil unrest and terrorism by paramilitary 'godfathers' (Powell, 1982).

The Black Report

The report of the review committee chaired by Sir Harold Black was published in 1979. The political and civil unrest, and the associated violence, had left Northern Ireland with the highest levels of social deprivation in the United Kingdom (Evason, 1978). The committee recognised that children's behaviour was affected by the environment in which they lived, and that the experience of poverty and serious deprivation had an impact on children's life chances and social behaviour. Despite the situational complexities caused by the political unrest the committee concluded that:

> The essential features of our strategy are prevention and co-ordination. Where problems do occur we advocate early and accurate identification and our approach is to seek support for children through the family, school and community, requiring co-operation and communication between parents and children, between families and the community, and between the wide range of voluntary and statutory agencies which have responsibility to help children and to prepare them for adult life. (Department of Health and Social Services, 1979, para. 9.3)

The Kincora scandal

The recommendations of the *Black Report* received a warm welcome from most professional groupings, but were overshadowed in April 1980 when three male members of staff from the Kincora Boys' Home in Belfast were charged with a number of offences relating to the systematic sexual and physical abuse of children in their care over a number of years. All three were later convicted and imprisoned. As early as 1967 there had been written complaints from two residents of Kincora alleging abuse by staff. These allegations appear to have been viewed as malicious and were subsequently dismissed. Over the next thirteen years further allegations and complaints were either unsubstantiated or disregarded, highlighting the inadequacy of the safeguards for children in state care. Following the convictions in 1980 allegations continued to be made that elements of the security services, civil servants and a number of loyalist paramilitaries had colluded and covered up the abuse of young boys at Kincora, as one of those convicted, William McGrath, was the leader of a loyalist paramilitary group called Tara, and rumours persisted that the security services had been employing McGrath as an informer (Moore, 1996).

In January 1982 the then Secretary of State for Northern Ireland, James Prior, established a Committee of Inquiry into the events surrounding Kincora. This inquiry collapsed, however, when three of the five panel members resigned, claiming that the police had not dealt with all the major criminal matters surrounding the case. Following debates in the Northern Ireland Assembly in 1983 about Kincora, the Secretary of State announced a full public inquiry under Judge William Hughes into the care of children residing in nine children's homes. The inquiry produced fifty-six recommendations that foreshadowed many of the conclusions of future inquiries which would take place in the other parts of the United Kingdom and Ireland into the care of children living away from home (Department of Health and Social Services, 1986). The Hughes recommendations emphasised the importance of:

- the management, supervision, monitoring and inspection of children's homes;

- the recognition of the roles and responsibilities between the statutory sector and voluntary organisations, who at the time, were a main provider of children's residential care;

- the need for a robust and independent complaints procedure for children in care and their parents;

- the need for effective recruitment and selection procedures for residential workers;

- parity of pay between residential and fieldwork social workers, linked to professional qualifications and training;

- the need to enhance the status of residential child care staff by ensuring that all officers in charge held a social work qualification, and that a timetable be established for ensuring that all care staff held suitable qualifications.

This final recommendation has resulted in Northern Ireland having the highest levels of training for residential child care workers across the United Kingdom (DHSSPS, 2003a).

The Hughes Report had a significant impact on the development of internal and external arrangements for supervising and monitoring children's residential homes in Northern Ireland. It was only later that similar issues in other parts of the United Kingdom were given the same attention (Utting, 1991; 1997).

The professionalisation of child protection

In 1989 the Department of Health and Social Services issued more comprehensive and prescriptive guidance on the management of child protection cases in *Co-operating to Protect Children* (HSS(CC)4/89). In contrast to
previous guidance which had run to six pages, the new guidance was over
seventy pages long and, mirroring the English and Welsh guidance (Department of Health and Social Security and Welsh Office, 1988), included, for
the first time, standard definitions of the different main types of abuse and
neglect, the roles and responsibilities of various professionals and agencies,
and detailed guidance on the handling of individual cases. This guidance
was underpinned by the roll-out of multidisciplinary in-service child protection training for health and social care professionals, aimed at supporting individuals to be more confident and competent at recognising the signs
and symptoms of abuse, and understanding their role in working with other
professionals.

One of the main consequences of the guidance was the establishment of
four Area Child Protection Committees within each Health and Social Services Board area, to replace the Area Review Committees (Department of
Health and Social Services, 1983) that were perceived as ineffectual and lacking in focus. A major criticism arising from a number of the child protection
inquiries conducted across the United Kingdom up to this time (Department
of Health and Social Security, 1982; Department of Health, 1991) was the
poor communication and ineffective coordination, and on occasions cooperation, between agencies as well as individual practitioners. The establishment of Area Child Protection Committees was seen as one way of tackling
this issue by bringing senior staff from different agencies and disciplinary
backgrounds together to oversee the strategic development and coordination
of child protection services.

An abuse of trust

The consequence of Kincora was a tightening of the processes for the
recruitment, selection and supervision of staff working in both children's
residential homes and the wider statutory sector. However, it soon became
apparent that individuals who posed a risk to children were still seeking
access to children in other ways. In 1992 Martin Huston was convicted on
twenty-five charges of the sexual abuse of six boys aged between 9 and 13
years. Huston already had convictions for the sexual abuse of children but
had moved between a number of voluntary and statutory organisations to

gain access to children as a volunteer. The report of a subsequent inquiry, *An Abuse of Trust*, published in December 1993, highlighted the need for voluntary organisations, and those providing services to children in the arts, sporting and faith sectors, to strengthen the arrangements for the vetting and employment of both paid and unpaid staff, and for greater compliance with child protection procedures (Department of Health and Social Services, 1993).

The Children (Northern Ireland) Order 1995

The enactment of the Children (Northern Ireland) Order 1995 in November 1996 was hailed as 'one of the most significant pieces of social legislation of the 20th century in Northern Ireland' (Department of Health, Social Services and Public Safety, 2003a, p. 13). Modelled on the Children Act 1989, and reflecting many of the principles underpinning the United Nations Convention on the Rights of the Child, the Order sought to strike a better balance between supporting parents in carrying out their parental responsibilities and greater judicial oversight of social workers' powers whenever parents were felt to be unable or unwilling to fulfil their responsibilities towards their children.

The new legislation strengthened the position of child care authorities by 'imposing a duty to investigate whether to take action to safeguard a child rather than solely to bring a child before a court if they were in need of care, protection or control' (Department of Health, Social Services and Public Safety, 2003a, p. 168). These duties were underpinned by a framework for planning children's services on an interagency basis in order to develop more universal and preventative services to support children and their families (McTernan and Godfrey, 2006).

The inspection of child protection services in Northern Ireland

The introduction of this new legislation and the learning arising from the Department of Health's *Messages from Research* (Department of Health, 1995) programme in England resulted in the issue of new child protection guidance, *Co-operating to Safeguard Children* (Department of Health, Social Services and Public Safety, 2003b). The guidance was broadly similar to *Working Together to Safeguard Children* (Department of Health *et al.*, 1999) and set out the role and expectations of professionals and agencies in relation to the protection of children from abuse and neglect. This coincided with the publication of the review into the death of Victoria Climbié

(Laming, 2003), which, while primarily focused on the English child protection system, held many key lessons for services and practices in Northern Ireland as well. One of the recommendations in the inquiry report was that agencies should conduct an audit of their child protection services against the key themes identified in the inquiry. The Department commissioned such a review in Northern Ireland in 2004, and the subsequent audit highlighted shortcomings in a number of areas (Department of Health, Social Services and Public Safety, 2006). As a consequence the Department embarked on an inspection of child protection arrangements and services in Northern Ireland. The inspection was undertaken in five of the eleven community Health and Social Services Trusts between 2004 and 2006. To assist with the inspection a set of draft standards was developed against which to assess services.

The findings from the inspection were similar to those from other inquiries, research and reviews conducted in Northern Ireland and elsewhere (for example, see Devaney, 2009; Hayes and Spratt, 2009). The benefit of a whole system inspection was that it confirmed what was previously suspected about the level of consistency in delivering children's services (Spratt, 2000). It revealed inconsistency in structures, roles, systems, processes and approaches.

The inspection was also critical of the quality of management of some children's services and identified poor assessment practice, a lack of critical review of cases, poor risk management and poor recording practices. There was wide acceptance of the recommendations of the report and a recognition of the need for change in order to fully realise the benefits of the integrated health and social care system for safeguarding children. It was also acknowledged that there was a real opportunity to achieve coherence in approaches due to the size of Northern Ireland and the close working relationships that existed between agencies.

The inspection report made seventy-seven recommendations. It was hoped that these would:

- improve arrangements for safeguarding children;
- increase public awareness and confidence in this important area;
- enhance professional practice, multidisciplinary and interagency working and service provision;
- inform policy development with regard to safeguarding children and young people.

While there was acceptance of the conclusions of the inspection, there was criticism of the inspection process itself. The inspection was originally scheduled to be completed within a year, but the illness of one of the key members of the inspection team resulted in the review taking nearly three years to be completed. In this time a number of factors arose that impacted on the remit and conduct of the inspection (Department of Health, Social Services and Public Safety, 2006). For example, in September 2004 the Northern Ireland Commissioner for Children and Young People raised the issue of the number of unallocated child care cases held by social services with the Minister. The inspection team was therefore asked to take this issue into account and to assess a number of unallocated/waiting list cases to ascertain if they had been screened appropriately to confirm the absence of child protection or other issues warranting urgent allocation. In 2005 concerns about the interface between residential and fieldwork services resulted in two of the five Health and Social Services Trusts having additional inspections undertaken of their children's residential homes, exploring the issue of how risks that children posed to other young people in residential care were managed.

In total the inspection process resulted in 792 local recommendations for the five Trusts inspected, in addition to the seventy-seven regional recommendations. Beyond the sheer number of recommendations that each organisation had to deal with was the fact that large numbers of action points dealt with similar issues; there was an overlap between local and regional recommendations; and the recommendations were sufficiently differentiated to require different action to be taken. This had the effect of creating a whole industry of activity involved in developing actions plans and implementing changes, causing an unparalleled level of change at a time of significant structural change within Northern Ireland.

Reform of public administration

In 2007 public services in Northern Ireland underwent their first major reform since the imposition of direct rule in 1972. The Review of Public Administration was designed to reduce bureaucracy and administration costs, renew local government and provide greater consistency in the delivery of public services to the Northern Ireland population. Health and social care was the first sector to reform its structures. The four Health and Social Services Boards were replaced by one Health and Social Care Board as the commissioner of services, and eighteen hospital and community health and social services Trusts were replaced by five integrated Health and Social Care Trusts, providing a mixture of community and hospital-based services.

The Reform Implementation Team

As a consequence of the child protection inspection the Minister for Health and Social Services endorsed the commencement of a reform programme led by the establishment of a Reform Implementation Team (www.dhssp-sni.gov.uk/index/ssi/oss-childrens-services.htm). The Team was designed to take forward the implementation of the recommendations of the child protection inspection and the associated developments required to improve services to children. This included bringing forward a Safeguarding Board for Northern Ireland to replace the four existing Area Child Protection Committees, supported by Local Safeguarding Panels within each of the five new Trusts.

The vision statement for the work of the Reform Implementation Team was: 'to create children's services that are acknowledged as being high quality, accessible, well managed and appropriately meeting need with a focus on improving outcomes for children'.

The process was managed as a project overseen by a Project Reference Group with the remit to oversee the implementation process and to endorse actions on a multi-agency basis. The group comprised senior managers from all the key agencies with representatives from the Department of Health, Social Services and Public Safety, the Department of Education, the Police Service of Northern Ireland, the Probation Board for Northern Ireland, the Youth Justice Agency and the voluntary sector. A multi-agency Implementation Group was established with responsibility for taking forward the actions required to implement the recommendations through a series of task-specific workstreams. These have evolved as key actions have been achieved and new areas of development work have been identified and agreed.

Funding was made available to each Health and Social Care Trust, as the lead agency, to recruit a Change Co-ordinator. This provided a necessary resource to support the local Project Teams within each Trust to coordinate actions and implement the recommendations on a multi-agency basis at local level, ensuring that actions were taken forward within the agreed timescales.

A fundamental principle underpinning implementation has been the need to ensure that it is an iterative process endeavouring to get feedback from front-line staff at every stage. This has helped to ensure that the reform is impacting on professional practice and that the work is shaped and formed by practitioner experience.

Gateway Teams

The Reform Implementation Process has sought to ensure greater standardisation of services and processes across the five new Health and Social Care Trusts. For example, Gateway Teams, established in each Trust, act as the front door to services for children and families with a published single point of contact (Department of Health, Social Services and Public Safety, 2008a). The objective is to improve the initial assessment of referrals by having these completed by experienced social work practitioners. Each team follows a common construct and is supported by Principal and Senior Practitioners who provide expert advice to staff and manage the most complex of referrals. The staffing complement includes newly qualified social workers who are in their assessed year in employment (AYE) (a grade to be introduced in England (Social Work Task Force, 2009)), with a ratio of one AYE per two qualified social workers where there is a Senior Practitioner in post within the team.

The Gateway staff undertake initial assessments prior to transferring the cases to specialist teams or signposting to other services. The teams operate within agreed regional protocols to ensure consistent approaches and to facilitate transfer of cases within given timescales.

UNOCINI

This approach was underpinned by the introduction of UNOCINI (*Understanding the Needs of Children in Northern Ireland*), a common assessment framework for social work that is increasingly being adopted by other agencies (Department of Health, Social Services and Public Safety, 2008d). The principles upon which UNOCINI is based are:

- assessment is an activity undertaken *with* the child and their family;
- assessments build on the strengths of families to meet the needs of their children;
- assessments are child-centred and rooted in child development;
- assessments are knowledge-based and show the evidence that underpins the assessment;
- they incorporate an assessment of any risk factors.

In terms of working with families and maintaining a focus on children, the first two principles may on the surface appear simplistic. However, this is complex work and the challenge has been to achieve this balance, particularly where there are safeguarding concerns (Horwath, 2007).

The UNOCINI Framework sets out a number of assessment pathways. All of the pathways have significant complementarities, dealing with strengths, needs, resilience and protective factors and include an assessment of risks. The pathways comprise:

- initial assessment;
- family support pathway;
- child protection pathway;
- looked after children pathway;
- leaving care pathway.

The framework is underpinned by and prompts practitioners to consider the United Nations Convention on the Rights of the Child. Upon completion each pathway must be quality assured by the designated manager. The pathways afford an opportunity for children and families to comment on the pathway and their experience of the interventions along that pathway. In essence the description of the pathways reflects the continuum of interventions a child might experience. However, the inclusion of the family support pathway reflects a commitment to identify a family's needs at an earlier stage and to ensure that appropriate services are available, rather than waiting for situations to worsen before intervening.

There are twelve identified domains of UNOCINI similar to other assessment frameworks (for example, Buckley, Horwath and Whelan, 2006; Department of Health, 2000) focusing on three key areas:

- child's needs: for health and development; education and learning; identity, self esteem and self care; family and social relationships;
- parents' or carers' capacity to meet the child's needs: basic care; ensuring safety; emotional warmth; guidance; boundaries; stimulation and stability;
- family and environmental factors: family history, functioning and well-being; extended family, social and community resources; housing; employment and income.

The framework provides a format for a preliminary assessment that can be undertaken by any professional within any agency. The objective is to facilitate an accumulation of information known about a child or family with a view to assessing the need for referral to social services. The development of a framework of thresholds of need (Department of Health, Social Services and Public Safety, 2008e) and thresholds of intervention (Department of Health, Social Services and Public Safety, 2008c) allows the professional and/or agency to consider what further supports and interventions they can offer, before they consider the necessity of referral to social services. These assessments are now increasingly being deployed by schools and education facilities, youth justice, and probation as well as individual health and social care practitioners. Utilising these assessments for referral to social services should lead to an improvement in the quality of information received by Gateway Teams and therefore more robust analysis and prioritisation of referrals.

Further work is being undertaken to look at the application of the family support pathway in assessing and meeting the needs of children with disabilities and their families, bearing in mind that these parents are not failing in their parenting capacity but they often need support and assistance to continue to care for their children, who have complex needs. On occasion other specialist assessments will be required and these should complement the UNOCINI assessment. A number of research-based assessment models have been identified with a view to achieving endorsement of standardised assessment tools to be used across Northern Ireland in areas such as parental substance misuse, domestic violence and parental mental illness. Work is also underway to develop e-documentation to allow for electronic referrals and transfer of information. A single regional Child Protection Register has been established and the e-documentation is due for roll out in 2010.

Implementation of UNOCINI has been supported by a multidisciplinary/multi-agency training programme utilising training material specially developed by the NSPCC. Following dialogue with the academic institutions in Northern Ireland, the reform measures and particularly the assessment framework have been assimilated into the teaching on the undergraduate social work degree.

Policies and procedures

A fundamental objective of the reform programme is to achieve consistency in the delivery of services to children and families. This aspiration is supported by the development of regionally agreed policies, procedures and protocols, which have been welcomed by practitioners. In addition to the above the range of measures includes:

- supervision policy, standards and criteria;
- administrative systems, recording policy, standards and criteria;
- quality assurance and performance management guidance, standards and criteria;
- caseload management model.

The development of these measures fulfil the recommendations of the child protection inspection report, and are subject to on-going review and evaluation to ensure that the experiences of their implementation and use inform their future refinement. They have been issued by the Department of Health and Social Services and Public Safety and are available on their website, www.dhsspsni.gov.uk/index/ssi/oss-childrens-services.htm.

Further work has been undertaken to develop an agreed interdisciplinary and interagency information-sharing policy and at the time of writing this is currently being consulted upon. The policy has been developed with multi-agency involvement and deals with the issues of consent and confidentiality, in particular raising the issue of the interface between human rights, the rights of children and the requirements of The Children (Northern Ireland) Order 1995.

The impact of child deaths

The above developments have been welcomed as both timely and constructive responses to the challenges faced by professionals and agencies in delivering child protection services. However, the context within which services are delivered is not static, and events can rapidly overshadow the progress being made.

While the public uproar surrounding the deaths of Victoria Climbié and Peter Connelly in England have impacted on political and professional consciousness in Northern Ireland, locally the deaths of children in two families have cast a long shadow over child protection in recent years.

On 12 July 2005 Mrs Madeleine O'Neill took her daughter Lauren's life and then her own. At the time of her death Lauren was 9 years old. According to the inquiry into the deaths (Western and Eastern Health and Social Services Boards, 2007), Mrs O'Neill told her GP, a private counsellor and a psychiatrist about her plan to kill her daughter and take her own life in the weeks preceding the deaths. However, despite this no one alerted social services or informed Mrs O'Neill's estranged husband to give him the opportunity to protect his daughter.

In a second case Arthur McElhill, a convicted sex offender, set fire to his home in November 2007, killing his partner Lorraine McGovern and their five children when he believed that his partner was intending to leave him. Two subsequent inquiries into the murders concluded that professionals could not have predicted the deaths, but that there were serious shortcomings in the way health professionals, criminal justice agencies and social workers enacted their child protection and public protection responsibilities (Department of Health, Social Services and Public Safety, 2008b; Northern Ireland Sex Offender Strategic Management Committee, 2008).

When a child dies and abuse or neglect is suspected, there has been a tension between public, political and professional perspectives about the causal factors and the remedial action required. As noted by Ayre (2001), this tension leads to the 'unholy trinity' of media pillorying, detailed post mortem recommendations about the operation of the system on the heels of inquiries, and the increasing prescription of practice, resulting in social workers and other child welfare professionals becoming focused on the need to avoid a non-accidental death which is the 'classic instance of a low probability/high consequence risk that leads to risk-averse cultures and practices in all walks of life' (Cooper *et al.*, 2003, pp. 10–11).

Both of these tragedies have resulted in extensive reviews of interagency and multidisciplinary working, and a heightened public concern about the effectiveness of the systems for keeping children safe. This has continued to be reflected in the public and media furore surrounding other child deaths, such as the suspected murder of another infant in December 2009 (*Belfast Telegraph*, 14 December 2009).

Conclusion

During the past forty years more than 3600 individuals have died as a result of the political unrest in Northern Ireland, with many tens of thousands of children and adults physically and psychologically scarred by the experiences they have endured (Eames and Bradley, 2009). Given this background it might seem that matters relating to the welfare of children might attract less attention from the public, politicians and professionals than they do in the other parts of the United Kingdom. Thankfully this has not been so, and children's issues have remained a central concern within civil and political society.

While Northern Ireland has had the highest levels of child poverty of any region within the United Kingdom during the majority of the past forty years (Hillyard *et al.*, 2003), it has had the lowest levels of public funding of statutory child welfare services across the four countries. For example, during 2004–5 the expenditure on personal social services was approximately £287 per child aged 0–17 years. This was 29% less than children's personal social services expenditure in England, 33% less than the equivalent expenditure in Wales and 44% less than that spent in Scotland (Economic Research Institute for Northern Ireland, 2007). This has compromised some of the possibilities for services developing more preventative and supportive approaches to the needs of children and families, alongside the necessary systems and services for responding to child protection concerns.

The imposition of Direct Rule in 1972 has resulted in Northern Ireland paralleling many of the developments regarding the safeguarding of children taking place in England. This has not necessarily been a bad thing, but it has had some unintended consequences. For example, there has until recently been a lack of attention from a succession of direct rule administrations to the cross-border dimension of child protection within an all-island context. This situation is now improving thanks to the North South Ministerial Council, one of the features of the Belfast Agreement and the Northern Ireland Act 1998, particularly in respect of the movement of adult sex offenders (Devaney and Reid, 2009).

As is the case in the rest of the United Kingdom professionals have struggled to find the right balance between supporting families during times of crisis and need, and stepping in whenever parents are either unable or unwilling to fulfil their parental responsibilities. While much of the professional practice regarding the protection of children is robust and effective, there remain concerns that this is not always the case. Therefore the recent reforms of the wider child welfare system in Northern Ireland are to be welcomed as a systemic and comprehensive approach to developing the best of what we already have, and ensuring that the framework is in place to enable practitioners and managers to undertake the work with children and their families that will deliver against the intended outcomes of a good child protection system.

At a time when the very notion of a United Kingdom is under review with the outworking of devolution in Scotland, Wales and Northern Ireland, there is the very real possibility that the structures and processes for keeping children safe will follow very different paths in each country. However it is to be hoped that while this experiment unfolds policy makers and academics will continue to share their experiences and collaborate over issues that are common regardless of borders.

CHAPTER 5

Getting it Right for Every Child in Scotland

Maggie Tierney, Christine Knight, Anne Stafford

Introduction

The subject of this chapter is child protection reform in Scotland. We begin by briefly describing the development of the modern child protection system in Scotland from the 1960s. Our main focus is, however, the period from 2000 during which Scotland underwent unprecedented change, including the introduction of a three-year Child Protection Reform Programme. Since the completion of the Child Protection Reform Programme policy emphasis has broadened from 'child protection' towards integrated support for children under a set of principles called *Getting it Right for Every Child* (GIRFEC); this chapter discusses the key elements of the GIRFEC approach.

First, it may be worth highlighting that, as for the other devolved countries of the UK, it is difficult to discuss any area of public policy development in Scotland without reference to our larger neighbour, England. For example, while there is growing Scottish research relating to children and child protection, until now much of the research base used in Scotland has been generated in England and based on the English system (Tarara and Daniel, 2007); and whereas high profile child death cases in Scotland make little impact on the child protection system in England, the reporting of English cases in Scotland can lead to considerable shifts in policy and practice.

History and development of child protection in Scotland 1960–2000

As in England, the 1950s and 1960s in Scotland saw developments in key elements of the child protection system that remain recognisable today. There was a similarly increasing role for the state in protecting children, a shift in responsibility from the voluntary sector to the state, and a move towards keeping families together rather than removing children from home.

Crucially, the period also saw the introduction of the distinctive Children's Hearing System that set Scotland's care and protection system apart from other systems in the UK. The Hearing System emerged following the recommendations of the Kilbrandon Committee, which had been set up in response to public concern about juvenile delinquency and crime (Scottish Executive, 2004 [1964]). The Committee considered arrangements for juveniles who were in need of care and protection or beyond parental control, concluding that both types of case should be dealt with in one system (Scottish Executive, 2004 [1964]).

A key principle underlying the Committee's work was that delinquency was the result of inadequate parental care and could only be dealt with by addressing the child's needs alongside the needs of his or her family (Scottish Executive, 2004 [1964]. The role of the court in cases was, and remains, confined to establishing facts where these are disputed. Thus an aspiration of the Scottish system from the 1960s was to embed child protection within a wider system of child welfare.

To date, the role of the hearing system has remained little changed since it was set up. However, a new Draft Children's Hearings Bill was published in June 2009 and following consultation the Bill will be introduced to the Scottish Parliament in early 2010. The reforms are aimed at strengthening and modernising the system, while retaining the ethos and principles of the original Children's Hearings System.

The Kilbrandon Committee report led directly to the 1968 Social Work (Scotland) Act, which located responsibility for child protection with newly created local authority social work departments and gave them statutory responsibility to take action where there was reasonable cause to suspect significant harm (Stafford and Vincent, 2008).

The 1970s and 1980s saw a series of scandals and high profile child death inquiries. These took place mainly in England but their repercussions were also felt in Scotland. Social work departments were criticised for not intervening enough to protect children and there were calls for a more interventionist approach. Early in the period the *Report of the Committee of Inquiry into the Care and Supervision Provided in Relation to Maria Colwell*, which led to changes in England, also had a profound effect in Scotland (Murray and Hill, 1991; Department of Health and Social Security, 1974) where there were parallel developments. The resulting Scottish Office Circular (Social Work Services Group, 1975) provided guidance to local authorities on setting up the case conference system, child abuse registers and Area Review Committees. However, at a time when England had many high profile child death cases, these were notably lacking in Scotland. This has been partly attributed to the smaller population; also perhaps to a different way of managing child deaths in Scotland, mainly through internal inquiry (Murray and Hill, 1991). While English cases at the time came under intense media scrutiny, there was less scrutiny in Scotland and a slightly different policy response.

In the 1980s and 1990s there were other inquiries and high profile cases that shifted the impetus for system change in another direction. Events in Cleveland in England and Orkney in Scotland in 1989 focused on public concern about the extent of social work powers to intervene in family life. This resulted in measures to increase accountability and transparency. The period also brought new awareness of child sexual abuse alongside neglect and physical abuse. There was increased impetus for legislative change and six years after reform of child care law in England, new legislation was passed in Scotland in 1995.

The Children (Scotland) Act 1995 remains the main legislative framework for children in Scotland (Scottish Office, 1995). It increased professional accountability and introduced a clear legal basis for professional intervention in family life to protect children. It attempted to ensure that the rights of children to be protected were more balanced towards the need to work in partnership with parents. Lord Clyde in the *Orkney Report* (1992) had been critical of the scope for discretion given to social work to intervene in family life to protect children. The Act attempted to define and regulate the powers and duties of local authorities and other agencies to intervene. New transparency and accountability were brought into the system and new duties were placed on local authorities to provide support to children in need in a preventive way.

There were new developments towards the latter part of the decade to regulate for the safety of children in residential care; and events in Dunblane (and later in Soham) graphically highlighted the risks children may face from unsuitable adults in the community. These were also a catalyst for policy and legislative development in Scotland and throughout the UK (Cullen, 1996; Bichard, 2004).

Child protection reform 2000 to the present day

Devolution and the socio-political context

Before discussing developments in child protection in Scotland from 2000, it may be useful to consider changes in the socio-political environment occurring at the time and in particular the impact of devolution on children's services and child protection. Since 1999 the Scottish Government has had responsibility for most aspects of child protection including social work, education, health and police. With this came new possibilities for Scotland and the other devolved countries to develop their own distinctive systems and mechanisms for protecting children.

However, while the effect of devolution on developing autonomous and distinctive policy and legislation is significant, it should not be overestimated. Scotland's ability to effect policy and legislation was not new. Prior to devolution the Scottish Office already acted remarkably autonomously from the UK government, particularly in most areas of social policy excluding social security and pensions. Brown *et al.* (1998) refer to an indigenous policy community and civil society with considerable scope for formulating legislation, developing policy and monitoring its implementation well before devolution.

Constitutional academics have observed that devolution is a process, not a policy (Sandford, 2005), and as the meaning of devolution continues to unfold, and different policy areas test its boundaries, the scope of real differences between Scotland and the rest of the UK remains to be seen. While child protection policy per se is fully devolved, even here there are policy challenges and opportunities. For example, there are interesting challenges around areas where there are cross-border issues. Child safety and the internet is an area of policy reserved to the UK government as it applies in Scotland, as is the issue of children of asylum-seeking families. In relation to vetting and barring arrangements, Scotland has its own legislation—the Protection of Vulnerable Groups (Scotland) Act 2007. However, it is also vital that Scotland works closely with other UK partners to avoid creating safe havens within the UK for those who would seek to harm children or vulnerable adults (Scottish Executive, 2007).

The current administration in Scotland has been a single-party SNP minority government since 2007, with the Scottish National Party currently holding a little over a third of the seats in the Scottish Parliament. One consequence of this is that this administration, more so perhaps than others with a parliamentary majority, needs to actively seek cross-party consensus on its major policy agendas. This is nowhere more true than in the area of services to protect children.

Another consequence of the SNP government is the now open discussion of an independence agenda for Scotland. This is a distinct thread of policy thinking within the Scottish Government, being explored through the National Conversation (Scottish Government, 2009). Even in policy areas like child protection where the whole of the UK clearly seeks similar good outcomes for children at risk, the National Conversation is providing an opportunity to test the strategy for achieving those outcomes within an independent Scotland. The vision in Scotland for protecting children may share many key characteristics with the vision held in England, Wales and Northern Ireland, but it remains a distinctly Scottish vision.

A third aspect of the current operating environment is the economic downturn, which demands political and social as well as economic adaptations. Again, this is not unique to Scotland, although facets of the way it manifests itself may be. For example, every government in the UK is observing closely the effect of the recession on vulnerable children and families and seeking to mitigate any increased risks. At a more strategic level, reduced public spend into the next few years strengthens the necessity across the whole public sector in Scotland to use available funds more efficiently and effectively in support of children and families at risk.

Scotland's size is another factor. With eight police forces, thirty-two local authorities and fourteen health boards, Scotland can, like the other devolved countries, with planning, bring all key partners together with greater assurance of inclusion and flexible participation than if our size and scale were larger. Like the other devolved countries, Scotland feels more networked and networkable.

Last, there is the deliberate transformative change being sought by the Scottish Government through its Concordat with local government, and onward locally through the Single Outcome Agreement (SOA) process. The government's purpose, as set out in the 2007 *Scotland Budget Spending Review*, is being pursued by consciously trying to alter the relationship between central government and the public sector by redistributing control and accountability to local level through Community Planning Partnerships (Scottish Government, 2007). *The National Performance Framework* sets out the fifteen national outcomes. Outcome No. 8, for example, states 'we have improved the life chances of children, young people and families at risk'. Each of the thirty-two local SOAs identifies how local partners agree priorities for their area. Unsurprisingly, the majority of the SOAs prioritise the protection of children at risk; and the findings of joint inspection of child protection services (as set out in *The Scotland Budget Spending Review* as one of the forty-five suggested national indicators) feature in many SOAs' performance measures (Scottish Government, 2007).

Child protection reform from 2000

Turning now to look at the recent history of child protection policy in Scotland, the period from 2000 until the present day has been a period of rapid, perhaps unprecedented, reform in Scotland. Child protection has received sustained political attention from successive governments.

A programme of child protection reform occurred in response to a major audit and review of the entire system in Scotland (Scottish Executive, 2002). The Audit and Review of Child Protection was announced following the publication of the Hammond review into the death of Kennedy McFarlane in Dumfries and Galloway (Scottish Executive 2002; Hammond 2001).

The audit and review led to the report *It's Everyone's Job to Make Sure I'm Alright*. The report identified some areas of good practice with regard to joint working and interagency communication, alertness to abuse and neglect, improvements in residential care, the introduction of a sex offenders register, and vetting arrangements (Scottish Executive, 2002).

It also identified significant weaknesses in the system in Scotland and in its ability to effect positive outcomes for children. It highlighted the high level of need experienced by some children in Scotland and concluded that in too many instances children did not receive the support they needed (Scottish Executive, 2002). Following the audit and review, a three-year programme of structural reform of services commenced and was informed by the following two guiding principles:

- that the effective protection of vulnerable children depends on good interagency working, especially, but not exclusively, across police, health and social work;
- that the rights of the child should be embedded into every aspect of delivery of services for, and with, the child.

Probably the strongest measures to emerge from the suite of activities undertaken during the three-year reform programme were:

- the *Children's Charter* (Scottish Executive, 2004a), a short statement of what children are entitled to expect from those who provide professional services to them;
- the *Framework for Standards* (Scottish Executive, 2004b), which set out how each of the terms in the Children's Charter should become enshrined into agencies' plans when delivering services to children at risk;
- the *Guidance to Child Protection Committees* (Scottish Executive, 2005), which set out the nine functions of the CPCs in Scotland, strengthening and clarifying their responsibilities for overseeing local multi-agency delivery of child protection services;
- the Joint Inspection of Children's Services (Scotland) Act (2006), which introduced a rigorous regime for concerted multi-agency inspection of services for children in Scotland, starting with child protection services.

The last of these will be discussed in some detail later in the chapter.

Getting it Right for Every Child (GIRFEC)

The Audit and Review of Child Protection in Scotland had made two main criticisms of the Children's Hearing System in Scotland (Scottish Executive, 2002). It was suggested that there existed several decision-making arenas for child protection in Scotland, which could be cumbersome, and that the Hearing System effectively added an additional layer when compared to systems in England and Wales and Northern Ireland.

In 2004 the Scottish Executive conducted the first major review of the Hearing System since the system was set up (Scottish Executive, 2004c). It was to take account of changes in the family, shifts in understandings of child abuse, and changes in the nature of referrals to the system (in 1976 care and protection cases accounted for 16% of referrals, in 2002 the proportion was 60%). The then Scottish Executive also highlighted growing concern about the effectiveness of the system with regard to outcomes for children (Scottish Executive, 2004c).

Following consultation, ministers concluded there was a need to take forward reform of the Children's Hearing System in the context of reform of children's services as a whole. The *Getting it Right for Every Child* proposals were introduced following the *Children's Hearing Review* (Scottish Executive, 2006).

The introduction of GIRFEC can be seen in the light of the considerable policy focus on children's issues over the whole of the preceding ten years and attempts to cumulatively address long-standing difficulties identified in successive reviews and inquiries in Scotland. Echoing the earlier aspirations of the Children's Hearing System, GIRFEC is a set of proposals for reform of children's services to improve outcomes for children by identifying need and intervening early. It is a strategy for streamlining children's services records, assessments and action plans, and for the development of national practice tools and guidance as well as electronic solutions to facilitate information sharing across children's services.

It places considerable emphasis on the joint responsibility of all agencies, including adult agencies, for the welfare and protection of children, and places greater emphasis on the responsibility of universal services such as education and health to deliver services to all children. It is based on the view that when given access to the help they need, many parents and children in difficulty can be effectively helped at an early stage and on a voluntary basis (Scottish Executive, 2002; 2006).

GIRFEC has identified eight areas of well-being in which children and young people need to progress in order to do well. These are supported by ten core components. The GIRFEC approach is one which promotes a shared approach and accountability that:

- builds solutions with and around children, young people and their families;
- enables children and young people to get the help they need when they need it;
- supports a positive shift in culture, systems and practice;
- involves working together to make things better. (Scottish Government, 2008, p. 10)

The ten core components that are central to GIRFEC and provide a benchmark from which practitioners may apply as an approach to their work are defined as:

- a focus on improving outcomes for children, young people and their families based on a shared understanding of well-being;
- a common approach to gaining consent and to sharing information where appropriate;

- an integral role for children, young people and families in assessment, planning and intervention;
- a coordinated and unified approach to identifying concerns, assessing needs, agreeing actions and outcomes, based on the well-being indicators;
- streamlined planning, assessment and decision-making processes that lead to the right help at the right time;
- consistent high standards of cooperation, joint working and communication where more than one agency needs to be involved, locally and across Scotland;
- a Lead Professional to coordinate and monitor multi-agency activity where necessary;
- maximising the skilled workforce within universal services to address needs and risks at the earliest possible time;
- a confident and competent workforce across all services for children, young people and their families;
- the capacity to share demographic, assessment and planning information electronically within and across agency boundaries through the national eCare programme where appropriate.

This approach is underpinned by common values and principles and by shared models, tools and practices to support work with children and young people. The values and principles are:

- promoting the well-being of individual children and young people;
- keeping children and young people safe;
- putting the child at the centre;
- taking a whole child approach;
- building on strengths and promoting resilience;
- promoting opportunities and valuing diversity;
- providing additional help that is appropriate, proportionate and timely;
- supporting informed choice;
- working in partnership with families;
- respecting confidentiality and sharing information;
- promoting the same values across the same working relationships;
- making the most of bringing together each worker's expertise;

- coordinating help;
- building a competent workforce to promote children and young people's well-being.

Getting it Right for Every Child also aims to build a network of support around each child or young person. The GIRFEC practice model consists of the *My World Triangle*, the eight well-being indicators and the *Resilience Matrix*.

GIRFEC is a national initiative, setting out a set of principles intended to apply nationally. In the context of the minority SNP administration's difficulty in passing national legislation, GIRFEC is being rolled out gradually across Scotland. It has currently been trialled and evaluated in a 'Pathfinder' project in Highland Region, and trialled in relation to the single issue of domestic abuse in four other local authority areas.

An evaluation of the development and early implementation phases of GIRFEC in Highland 2006–2009 acknowledged that organisational and workforce change on the scale required by GIRFEC would tend to be gradual and incremental but concluded that professional practice is changing in the desired way (Stradling *et al.*, 2009). The pilot evaluation in Highland indicated a large reduction in the number of referrals to the Children's Reporter, large reductions in numbers of children on the Child Protection Register, and a fall in referral rates. This indicates a more proportionate response to concerns, providing evidence that GIRFEC will relieve pressure on statutory services (Stradling *et al.*, 2009).

Inspecting child protection in Scotland

The joint inspection regime in Scotland has been a major driver for improvement in standards of services to protect children in Scotland since the Audit and Review of Child Protection and in the context of GIRFEC. There are a number of departures in content and method from the Ofsted inspections in England and this is worth discussing in some detail here.

Since 2004 in Scotland a programme of joint inspections of services to protect children has been developed and implemented by Her Majesty's Inspectorate of Education (HMIE). As an executive agency of the Scottish Government, HMIE works independently and impartially while remaining directly accountable to Scottish Ministers for the standard of its work. This ensures the independence of inspection and reporting within the overall context of Scottish Ministers' strategic objectives for Scotland.

HMIE works in partnership with services to achieve improvement through a combination of support and challenge. Developing services' own approaches to improvement through robust self-evaluation and planning for improvement is key to this approach. The inspection of services to protect children is based on a set of published quality indicators, *How Well are Children Protected and Their Needs Met?* (HM Inspectorate of Education, 2005). This is to encourage self-evaluation and ensure that the inspection process is transparent.

In January 2006, the Scottish Parliament introduced legislation, the Joint Inspection of Children's Services and Inspection of Social Work Services (Scotland) Act 2006, which provided the legal framework under which these inspections are carried out in Scotland. The legislation made provision 'requiring or facilitating the sharing or production of information (including medical records) for the purpose of an inspection'.

Between 2006 and 2009, all thirty-two local authority areas in Scotland were inspected and a report for each authority was published on the HMIE website. The methodology for the inspection is based on the experiences of a sample of children and their families in each area. The starting point is reviewing children's experience by reading case records. Up to seventy children were included in the sample in large authority areas, and around thirty in smaller authorities. In all, evidence was gathered from the records of up to 1700 children.

A sample of children and families was selected for even closer involvement. These families and all professionals working with them were invited to meet inspectors to talk about their experiences. Inspectors also conducted focus groups bringing together specialist and non-specialist staff. For example within police services, inspectors met family protection units. They also met officers involved in community policing or in drug squads.

Evidence from all aspects of inspection contributed to evaluations of the quality of outcomes for children and their experiences using the quality indicators. HMIE uses a six-point evaluation scale from excellent to unsatisfactory. In a number of areas, HMIE has returned to evaluate progress made on action points.

A full analysis of the first programme of inspections was published by HMIE in November 2009. Its findings showed that practice varies across the country. For example, evaluations for the quality indicator 'children's needs are met' and the related indicator 'effectiveness of planning to meet needs' vary from unsatisfactory to very good. These are fundamental aspects of protecting children, yet variation in relation to them is high. Risk assessment is another area of inconsistency. In many areas risk assessment tools are available, but staff are not always familiar with them or they may not use them. Comprehensive assessment of risk and needs is not widely or consistently used. In some areas there were delayed assessments, resulting in delays in decisions by the Children's Reporter, with subsequent negative consequences for children (HM Inspectorate of Education, 2009b).

Across the country children were found to have a good understanding of how to keep themselves safe, and could identify trusted adults they would go to if they had concerns. This reflects the attention given by professionals in schools and in other services to educational programmes on personal safety. While it is encouraging that children are able to report to inspectors that they know what to do if they have concerns, it does not provide evidence that they do it, or that they get the help they need when they do so (HM Inspectorate of Education, 2009b).

Public accountability related to a published inspection report has had an impact on how senior managers and elected members view their responsibilities. This has been helpful for operational managers across all services who have struggled to convince strategic managers and planners of the importance of their work, and the risks to children in their area.

Professional dialogue is an important part of the inspection process. It provides an opportunity for staff to talk about the successes and challenges of their work. Many staff involved in the inspections comment positively on this, finding it can increase their confidence and provide new insights. It helps develop a culture in organisations of reflective practice. Engaging staff from different services all working with a single family can also encourage reflection across services and contribute to breaking down professional barriers.

Linking the inspection process to self-evaluation has the potential to help services reflect on their practice and achieve improvement. Supported by the inspectorate, services are now beginning to develop their own approaches to self-evaluation. In the best examples, Child Protection Committees have taken a lead and used a small number of quality indicators to evaluate practice, starting with children's records.

Having completed a programme of inspection HMIE is now entering a second round of inspections, related to the *National Performance Framework*. Having achieved baseline information from across the country in the first programme, HMIE is now able to take forward a more proportionate approach. The quality indicators have been revised and published in *How Well Do We Protect Children and Meet their Needs?* (HM Inspectorate of Education, 2009a). The new inspection model will evaluate a smaller group of quality indicators, focusing on those which evaluate outcomes and experiences of children and their families. The inspection will be again based on a sample of children and their families in each area, but all children in the sample will be on the Child Protection Register or recently removed from it. This will mean that the process focuses more on the most vulnerable children and families. Inspectors will follow up every child in the sample, through meetings with the network of professionals supporting the child and when appropriate with the child and family. All children and their families who are on the Child Protection Register will also be invited to complete a questionnaire about their experiences.

The inspection and regulatory landscape in Scotland is currently undergoing further change. A new organisation will be set up in 2011 with responsibility for social work services and social care. Responsibility for inspection of services to protect children will, in future, lie with this new body.

The inspection programme has had a significant impact across services in Scotland. It has opened up practice across services. In an area of work that has tended to be examined only following critical incidents, it has allowed reporting on practice and engagement with professionals in the spirit of joint commitment to improvement. It has led to direct improvements in practice in some areas and has highlighted the often very high standard of work carried out by many professionals in this challenging and difficult field of work.

Beyond GIRFEC

Since the conclusion of the Child Protection Reform Programme in 2006–7 the Scottish Government has worked to bed in the new arrangements. This is being achieved in Scotland partly through the strengthened Child Protection Committees (CPCs). The thirty multi-agency CPCs, whose role has grown substantially in recent years, now comprise the principal stakeholder network for the Scottish Government in developing policies for the protection of children at risk (Scottish Executive, 2005).

A forum of quarterly discussions is organised by Scottish Government with the Chairs and Lead Officers of the thirty CPCs. It has enabled discussion and updating on subject-specific draft policies (e.g. young runaways, trafficked children), and for difficult practice issues to be progressed (e.g.

improving the recognition and assessment of risks to children, engaging the general public in taking action when they have concerns about a child, agreeing appropriate forms of information-sharing).

In contrast to the moves in England towards the language and practice of 'safeguarding', the non-statutory CPCs in Scotland retain a firm focus on services to protect children at risk of neglect or abuse. In light of recent structural changes announced in England following Baby Peter, there are strengths in retaining this highly focused child protection remit.

The Scottish Government's strategic challenge at this point is to manage the process of locating child protection practice within the maturing GIRFEC practice model in a way which is safe, robust, flexible and empowering to front-line child protection practitioners and their organisations. The government believes this ambition is not at odds with CPCs retaining clear and separate strategic responsibility and accountability for the quality of local multi-agency arrangements for protecting children at risk of harm.

Most recently, a national working group has been set up in Scotland to review the national child protection guidance – *Protecting Children: A Shared Responsibility* – which has been in place since 1998 (Scottish Office, 1998). This review will explicitly address findings from the inspection programme and significant case reviews in Scotland. In particular it is planned to strengthen guidance on assessment of risk and needs, information-sharing and operational planning. Arrangements for transfer of planning responsibilities and records of professional involvement with families across authority and national borders will be clarified. Scottish Ministers have also asked the review group to capture new sources of threat to children which will grow in ubiquity or seriousness in the next decade (e.g. keeping children safe in the online environment, or the management of risks to children affected by their parents' drug or alcohol misuse). The Review of the 1998 Guidance is expected to take about a year to draft and consult on, and a further year to give firm roots to embedding its revised terms into practice.

Conclusion

The setting up of the Children's Hearing System in the 1960s was a distinctive and bold attempt in Scotland to address the needs of children using a welfare-based approach that emphasised intervening early and supporting children alongside their parents. Since the outset, however, the aspirations of the Hearing System have, at times, sat rather uneasily alongside a child protection system in Scotland, which, like the rest of the UK, is narrowly investigative and procedurally focused.

The gradual rolling out of GIRFEC across Scotland, coupled with Scotland's innovative approach to child protection inspection and the recent work being carried out by the national group set up to review national child protection guidance, marks another new and bold attempt at transformative system change to children's services in Scotland. At this juncture, it remains to be seen whether this can be a genuinely new departure, able to effect real change, resolve old tensions inherent in the Scottish system, and create a system working harmoniously to deliver for all children in a way that ensures the needs of the most vulnerable are met.

CHAPTER 6

Safeguarding and protecting children across the UK: similar but distinctive systems

Anne Stafford, Sharon Vincent, Nigel Parton

In this concluding section we draw out and compare broad themes emerging from the chapters.

Each of the countries of the UK has over the past decade introduced major programmes of reform in children's services and, in particular, those services that safeguard and protect children and young people. What we have set out in the preceding chapters is a collection of reflections on these reforms provided by key individuals working in and familiar with at least one of the systems. Our aim was to describe recent developments in systems to safeguard and protect children in different parts of the UK, draw out key strands and emerging themes, reflect on similarities and differences between systems, and pull together an early assessment of what is happening to child protection across the UK in the context of devolution.

In the introduction we highlighted the importance of intra-country comparative research as an opportunity to raise our heads and use a wider perspective from which to consider our own system in the context of other systems. We quoted the famous Scottish (anti-)psychiatrist R. D. Laing:

> Comparison allows you to unpickle yourself from your place in the pickling jar and see that there is a different kind of life (quoted by Andrew Cooper in Hill *et al.*, 2002).

We suggested in the introduction that this 'unpickling' sits at the core of CLiCPs remit and the main focus of this book has been on learning from our near neighbours in different parts of the UK. Before we draw out emerging themes, and in the interests of further 'unpickling', it may be useful to raise our heads even further to consider UK systems to safeguard and protect children in an international context.

Since the 1990s, some writers on child protection have suggested that child protection systems throughout the world can be broken down into two broad types, with countries falling to a greater or lesser degree into one or other of them. These are first, systems in countries such as the UK, US and Australia, and second, systems of continental and northern Europe such as the Netherlands, Belgium and Sweden (Gilbert, 1997; Hill *et al.*, 2002; Stafford and Vincent, 2008; Gilbert *et al.*, 2010). Using these schematic categorisations, systems of the first type are said to be more narrowly focused on child protection, while the second emphasises protecting children within a broader system of child welfare and family support. While these are rather crude ideal types they are useful in our task of overviewing the different systems in the UK.

Thus, in the former UK, US, Australia type system, child protection is usually distinct from broader systems of child welfare and more closely merged with the criminal justice system. Thresholds for intervention ensure resources are targeted at high risk cases, and there is a history of such systems changing in response to public reaction to and inquiries into high profile cases (Gilbert, 1997; Hill *et al.*, 2002; Stafford and Vincent, 2008; Gilbert *et al.*, 2010).

In the type of system characteristic of continental and northern Europe the emphasis is more on prevention, early intervention and support to families delivered via universal services. Here, children are rarely removed from their families, parents tend to be less fearful of protection services, professionals tend to be more respected and they have a more positive public image than in systems more narrowly focused on child protection (Hill *et al.*, 2002; Stafford and Vincent, 2008).

At the time these models of child protection systems were elaborated, all of the child protection systems of the UK sat firmly within the former UK, US, Australia type model. They were narrowly focused on child protection, tightly procedurally specified, and rooted in adversarial legal systems (Hill *et al.*, 2002; Stafford and Vincent, 2008). While Scotland also sat within this model, its welfare-based Children's Hearing System placed it as more of a hybrid, its starting point for reform perhaps already closer to the systems of continental and northern Europe (Hill *et al.*, 2002; Stafford and Vincent, 2008).

In relation to this, and in the context of perhaps unprecedented reform of services to safeguard and protect children in the UK since 2000, we might ask ourselves the following questions. What has happened to the various systems of the UK in the context of devolution? What has been the overall effect of child protection reform across the UK? Where do the systems now sit along the child protection/family support continuum? Have they pushed the systems of the UK backwards along the continuum towards being more narrowly focused on child protection? Have the reforms pushed the systems forward towards the systems of continental and northern Europe with the emphasis on protecting children within a wider model of family support?

What is clear from earlier chapters in this book is that what our authors are describing are systems that remain broadly similar, and they retain much in common. We have seen that in each part of the UK reform of child protection is taking place within reform of children's services as a whole. In each part of the UK the aim of reform has been to increase the focus on prevention and emphasise the key role of universal services in identifying and intervening early to prevent harm by supporting vulnerable children and families. This perhaps demonstrates a shift across the UK along the continuum in the direction of systems of continental and northern Europe.

Across the UK, therefore, the general direction of travel is the same.

However, when we come to the level of the individual countries of the UK, the picture is more complex. While the direction may be one way, the routes taken have been different: neither uniform, linear nor smooth.

For example, Nigel Parton, Phillip Noyes and Wendy Rose described the effect on the English system of the death of Baby Peter in England. However, the impact of this was not evenly felt in each part of the UK. The death of Baby Peter was extensively reported throughout the UK via UK media. In England, system change as a result was significant. It was also, arguably, against the prevailing direction of travel, pushing the system to safeguard children in England back in the direction from where it came towards a more narrow focus on child protection. Whether this directional change is long-term and substantive, or temporary and a blip, remains to be seen.

This effect was not precisely replicated in other parts of the UK. The response to the death of Baby Peter in Scotland led to an explicit policy statement to hold firm to planned developments in children's services, and a few new initiatives were announced. In addition, around the same time as the Baby Peter case in England, Scotland had its own child death case: Brandon Muir died around the same time as Baby Peter in broadly similar circumstances. This also led to some change in Scotland but not of the same order as in England. Thus, while there was pressure for system change in response to the Baby Peter case in each part of the UK, the responses were different.

Earlier chapters also demonstrate that devolution has added a new dynamic to the mix of reform of policy and services to safeguard and protect children, more so in the three devolved countries. We are at early stages in understanding the process of devolution and how it will unfold. In relation to safeguarding and protecting children the dynamic is complex and hard to unravel. Our earlier chapters provide some information that in the three devolved countries there is growing awareness of new opportunities being afforded by devolution. They appear to be taking tentative steps to test and explore new solutions, looking to find more country-specific solutions to long-standing safeguarding and protection issues. These may increasingly reflect their national identities and local operating conditions and provide scope to develop in ways that are genuinely creative and locally relevant.

There seems to be increasing awareness that size matters, in that the smaller devolved countries may be able to open up opportunities for different kinds of change. The authors of Chapter 5 suggested that Scotland seems more networked and more networkable. This is illustrated in a number of chapters. For example, there is some information that the devolved areas are developing more national, centralised approaches. John Devaney, Fionnuala McAndrew and Tony Rodgers highlighted in Chapter 4 that in the context of the Northern Ireland Assembly Northern Ireland is in the midst of its biggest shake-up of public services in thirty years. Within these reforms, reform of children's services seems to be developing in a more centralised way than in other parts of the UK. Unlike other parts of the UK, Wales has recently introduced all-Wales child protection guidance, issued not by central government but under the auspices of the Area Safeguarding Children's Boards. All-Wales guidance has also been issued on conducting serious case reviews.

There is also evidence of moves in a different direction: towards decentralisation. In Scotland, the concordat between central government and the Convention of Scottish Local Authorities (COSLA) resulted in ring-fenced funds being devolved from central to local government. This marked a shift in the nature of the relationship between central and local government in Scotland, perhaps reflecting SNP commitment to local democracy. This is also perhaps evidenced in the GIRFEC approach being gradually rolled out across local authorities using a mix of persuasion and consensus.

Across the UK the process of reform of safeguarding and protecting children has been one of near neighbours developing separately but with some awareness of what is happening in other parts of the UK. For example, the architects of GIRFEC in Scotland began the process of reform of children's services some time after the reform of children's services in England. They were therefore able to take account of developments in England when shaping reform of the system in Scotland. The team responsible for developing the eCare system in Scotland spent time in England with the team developing the ContactPoint database in England, taking advantage of learning from early development of the system.

All of the devolved countries of the UK have taken account of research and findings from Serious Case Reviews in England in developing their systems. While the devolved countries might all look to England and take account of developments there, the opposite is not always the case, with England more likely to develop without reference to the devolved countries.

Thus, while the systems of the UK are broadly similar, they are also distinct. Each of the four parts has its own clear and separate vision for what they want to achieve for children, and a distinctive policy framework for achieving it. The factors driving change in systems are complex. They relate as much to wider political processes and the changing dynamics and relationships between countries as they do to factors solely concerned with safeguarding and protecting children.

We conclude by reiterating the paragraph that ends the Northern Ireland chapter. At a time when the very notion of a United Kingdom is under review with the outworking of devolution in Scotland, Wales and Northern Ireland, there is the very real possibility that the structures and processes for keeping children safe will follow very different paths in each country. It is to be hoped though that while this experiment unfolds, policy makers and academics will continue to share their experiences and collaborate over issues that are common regardless of borders.

References

Audit Commission (1994) *Seen But Not Heard: Coordinating Community Child Health and Social Services for Children in Need*, London: HMSO

Ayre, P. (2001) 'Child protection and the media: lessons from the last three decades', *British Journal of Social Work*, Vol. 31, No. 6, pp. 887–901

Belfast Telegraph (2009) 'Horrific last hours of 15-month-old Millie Martin's life', 14 December. Available from URL: www.belfasttelegraph.co.uk/news/local-national/horrific-last-hours-of-15monthold-millie-martins-life-14596954.html#ixzz0ch3NPqtk

Bichard, M. (2004) *The Bichard Inquiry Report*, London: The Stationery Office

Brown, A., McCrone, D. and Paterson, L. (1998) *Politics and Society in Scotland*, Basingstoke: Palgrave

Buckley, H., Horwath, J. and Whelan, S. (2006) *Framework for the Assessment of Vulnerable Children and their Families*, Dublin: Trinity College Dublin

Byrne, D. (2005) *Social Exclusion* (2nd edition), Buckingham: Open University Press

Care and Social Services Inspectorate Wales (2009a) *Annual Report 2007–2008*, Cardiff: CSSIW

Care and Social Services Inspectorate Wales (2009b) *Improving Practice to Protect Children in Wales: An Examination of the Role of Serious Case Reviews*, Cardiff: CSSIW

Care and Social Services Inspectorate Wales (2009c) *Safeguarding and Protecting Children in Wales: The Review of Local Authority Social Services and Local Safeguarding Children Boards*, Cardiff: CSSIW

Chief Secretary to the Treasury (2003) *Every Child Matters*, London: The Stationery Office

Children and Family Court Advisory and Support Service (2009) *CAFCASS Care Demand – Latest Quarterly Figures: 08 July 2009*, London: CAFCASS

Children, Schools and Families Committee (2009) *Third Report: Looked-after Children*, Vol. 1 (HC 111-1) and Vol. 2 (HC 787), session 2008–9. Available from URL: www.publications.parliament.uk/pa/cm200809/cmselect/cmchilsch/cmchilsch.htm#reports (accessed 23 February 2010)

Clyde, J. J. (1992) *The Report of the Inquiry into the Removal of Children from Orkney in February 1991*, Edinburgh: HMSO

Cooper, A., Hetherington, R. and Katz, I. (2003) *The Risk Factor – Making the Child Protection System Work for Children*, London: Demos

Corby, B., Doig, A. and Roberts, V. (1998) 'Inquiries into child abuse', *Journal of Social Welfare and Family Law*, Vol. 20, No. 4, pp. 377–95

Cullen, W. D. (1996) *The Public Inquiry into the Shootings at Dunblane Primary School on 13 March 1996*, London: The Stationery Office

Department for Children, Schools and Families (1999) *Children Looked After by Local Authorities. Year ending 31 March 1998, England*, London: DCSF

Department for Children, Schools and Families (2008) *Referrals, Assessments and Children and Young People who are the Subject of a Child Protection Plan, England – Year ending 31 March 2008*, London: DCSF

Department for Education and Skills (2004) *Every Child Matters: Next Steps*, London: DfES

Department of Health (1991) *Child Abuse: A Study of Inquiry Reports 1980–1989*, London: HMSO

Department of Health (1994) *Children Act Report 1993*, London: HMSO

Department of Health (1995) *Child Protection: Messages from Research*, London: HMSO

Department of Health (2000) *Framework for the Assessment of Children in Need and Their Families*, London: Department of Health

Department of Health (2001) *The Children Act Now: Messages from Research*, London: The Stationery Office

Department of Health (2002) *Safeguarding Children: A Joint Chief Inspectors' Report on Arrangements to Safeguard Children*, London: DOH

Department of Health, Home Office, and Department of Education and Employment (1999) *Working Together to Safeguard Children: A Guide to Inter-agency Working to Safeguard and Promote the Welfare of Children*, London: The Stationery Office

Department of Health and Social Security (1974) *Non-Accidental Injury to Children*, LASSL (74) 13

Department of Health and Social Security (1976a) *Non-Accidental Injury to Children: Area Review Committees*, LASSL (76) 2

Department of Health and Social Security (1976b) *Non-Accidental Injury to Children: The Police and Case Conferences*, LASSL (76) 26

Department of Health and Social Security (1978) *Child Abuse: The Register System*, LA/C396/23D

Department of Health and Social Security (1980) *Child Abuse: Central Register Systems*, LASSL (80) 4, HN (80)

Department of Health and Social Security (1982) *Child Abuse: A Study of Inquiry Reports 1973–1981*, London: HMSO

Department of Health and Social Security and Welsh Office (1988) *Working Together: A Guide to Arrangements for Inter-agency Co-operation for the Protection of Children from Abuse*, London: HMSO

Department of Health and Social Services (1979) *Report of the Children and Young Persons Review Group* (the Black Report), Belfast: HMSO

Department of Health and Social Services (1983) *Child Abuse Registers in Northern Ireland*, Belfast: Department of Health and Social Services

Department of Health and Social Services (1986) *Report of the Inquiry into Children's Homes and Hostels* (the Hughes Report), Belfast: HMSO

Department of Health and Social Services (1993) *An Abuse of Trust*, Belfast: Department of Health and Social Services

Department of Health, Social Services and Public Safety (2003a) *A Better Future: 50 Years of Child Care in Northern Ireland*, Belfast: DHSSPS

Department of Health, Social Services and Public Safety (2003b) *Co-operating to Safeguard Children*, Belfast: DHSSPS

Department of Health, Social Services and Public Safety (2006) *Our Children and Young People – Our Shared Responsibility: Inspection of Child Protection Services in Northern*

Ireland, Belfast: DHSSPS

Department of Health, Social Services and Public Safety (2008a) *Gateway Service – Processes: Guidance for Northern Ireland Health and Social Care Trusts*, Belfast: DHSSPS. Available from URL: www.dhsspsni.gov.uk/gateway_service___ processes___guidance_for_northern_ireland_health_and_social_care_trusts.pdf (accessed 13 January 2010)

Department of Health, Social Services and Public Safety (2008b) *Independent Review Report of Agency Involvement with Mr Arthur McElhill, Ms Lorraine McGovern and Their Children*, Belfast: DHSSPS

Department of Health, Social Services and Public Safety (2008c) *UNOCINI Family and Child Care: Thresholds of Intervention*, Belfast: DHSSPS. Available from URL: www. dhsspsni.gov.uk/family_and_child_care_thresholds_of_intervention.pdf (accessed 13 January 2010)

Department of Health, Social Services and Public Safety (2008d) *UNOCINI Guidance*, Belfast: DHSSPS. Available from URL: www.dhsspsni.gov.uk/unocini_guidance.pdf (accessed 13 January 2010)

Department of Health, Social Services and Public Safety (2008e) *UNOCINI Thresholds of Need Model*, Belfast: DHSSPS. Available from URL: www.dhsspsni.gov.uk/ thresholds_of_need_model.pdf (accessed 13 January 2010)

Devaney, J. (2009) 'Chronic child abuse: the characteristics and careers of children caught in the child protection system', *British Journal of Social Work*, Vol. 39, No. 1, pp. 24–45

Devaney, J. and Reid, C. (2009) 'Two countries, one border: the challenges and opportunities for protecting children on an all island basis – a critical turning point' Conference Paper, Keeping Children Safe – Critical Times, Critical Issues. Cork, 23rd October.

Eames, R. and Bradley, D. (2009) *The Report of the Consultative Group on the Past*. Available from URL: www.cgpni.org/ (accessed 12 January 2010)

Economic Research Institute for Northern Ireland (2007) *An Analysis of the Public Expenditure on Children in Northern Ireland*, Belfast: ERINI

Evason, E. (1978) *Family Poverty in Northern Ireland*, London: Child Poverty Action Group

Featherstone, B. (2004) *Family Life and Family Support: A Feminist Analysis*, Basingstoke: Palgrave Macmillan

France, A. and Utting, D. (2005) 'The paradigm of "risk and protection-focused prevention" and its impact on services for children and families', *Children and Society*, Vol. 19, No. 2, pp. 77–90

Franklin, B. and Petley, J. (1996) 'Killing the age of innocence: newspaper reporting of the death of James Bulger', in Pilcher, J. and Wagg, S. (eds) (1996) *Thatcher's Children? Politics, Childhood and Society in the 1980s and 1990s*, London: Falmer Press

Frost, N. and Parton, N. (2009) *Understanding Children's Social Care: Politics, Policy and Practice*, London: Sage

Gilbert, N. (ed.) (1997) *Combating Child Abuse: International Perspectives and Trends*, Oxford: Oxford University Press

Gilbert, N., Parton, N. and Skivenes, M. (eds) (2010) *Child Protection Systems: International Trends and Orientations*, New York: Oxford University Press

Hammond, H. (2001) *Child Protection Inquiry into the Circumstances Surrounding the Death of Kennedy McFarlane, d.o.b 17 April 1997*, Dumfries: Dumfries and Galloway

Child Protection Committee

Hayes, D. and Spratt, T. (2009) 'Child welfare interventions: patterns of social work practice', *British Journal of Social Work*, Vol. 39, No. 8, pp. 1575–97

Hendrick, H. (2003) *Child Welfare*, Bristol: Policy Press

Hill, M., Stafford, A. and Green-Lister, P. (eds) (2002) *International Perspectives on Child Protection*, Edinburgh: Scottish Executive

Hillyard, P., Kelly, G., McLaughlin, E., Patsios, D. and Tomlinson, M. (2003) *Bare Necessities: Poverty and Social Exclusion in Northern Ireland*, Belfast: Democratic Dialogue

HM Government (2004) *Every Child Matters: Change for Children*, London: The Stationery Office

HM Government (2006) *Working Together to Safeguard Children: A Guide to Interagency Working to Safeguard and Promote the Welfare of Children*, London: The Stationery Office

HM Government (2008) *Staying Safe: Action Plan*, London: Department for Children, Schools and Families

HM Government (2009) *The Protection of Children in England: Action Plan. The Government's Response to Lord Laming*, Cm 758, London: Department for Children, Schools and Families

HM Inspectorate of Education (2005) *How Well are Children and Young People Protected and their Needs Met?* Edinburgh: HMIE

HM Inspectorate of Education (2009a) *How Well Do We Protect Children and Meet their Needs?*, Edinburgh: HMIE

HM Inspectorate of Education (2009b) *How Well Do We Protect Scotland's Children? A Report on the Findings of the Joint Inspections of Services to Protect Children 2005–2009*, Edinburgh: HMIE

Home Office, Department of Health, Department of Education and Science, and the Welsh Office. (1991) *Working Together under the Children Act 1989: A Guide to Arrangements for Inter-agency Co-operation for the Protection of Children from Abuse*, London: HMSO

Horwath, J. (2007) 'Safeguarding children: the assessment challenges', in Wilson, K. and James, A. (eds) (2007) *The Child Protection Handbook* (3rd edition), London: Baillière Tindall

Horwath, J. (2009) 'Managing difference: working effectively in a multi-agency context', in Cleaver, H., Cawson, P., Gorin, S. and Walker, S. (eds) (2009) *Safeguarding Children: A Shared Responsibility*, Chichester: Wiley

Hudson, B. (2005) 'Partnership working and the children's services agenda: is it feasible?' *Journal of Integrated Care*, Vol. 13, No. 2, pp. 7–12

Hudson, B., Hardy, B., Henwood, M. and Wistow, G. (1999) 'In pursuit of interagency collaboration in the public sector: what is the contribution of theory and research?', *Public Management: An International Journal of Research and Theory*, Vol. 1, No. 2, 235–60

Kirton, D. (2008) *Child Social Work Policy and Practice*, London: Sage

Labour and Plaid Cymru Groups (2007) *One Wales: A Progressive Agenda for the Government of Wales*. Available from URL: www.plaidcymru.org/uploads/publications/281.pdf (accessed 23 February 2010)

Laming, Lord (2003) *The Victoria Climbié Inquiry: Report of an Inquiry by Lord Laming*, Cm 5730, London: The Stationery Office

Laming, Lord (2009) *The Protection of Children in England: A Progress Report*, London:

The Stationery Office

Levitas, R. (2005) *The Inclusive Society? Social Exclusion and New Labour* (2nd edition), Basingstoke: Palgrave Macmillan

Lindon, J. (2008) *Safeguarding Children and Young People: Child Protection 0–18 years*, London: Hodder Education

Local Government Association (2009) 'Councils struggling to recruit social workers in wake of Baby Peter' (online). Available from URL: www.lga.gov.uk/lga/core/page.do?pageId=1868480

London Borough of Brent (1985) *A Child in Trust: Report of the Panel of Inquiry Investigating the Circumstances Surrounding the Death of Jasmine Beckford*, London: London Borough of Brent

London Borough of Greenwich (1987) *A Child in Mind: Protection of Children in a Responsible Society. Report of the Commission of Inquiry into the Circumstances Surrounding the Death of Kimberley Carlile*, London: London Borough of Greenwich

London Borough of Lambeth (1987) *Whose Child? The Report of the Panel Appointed to Inquire into the Death of Tyra Henry*, London: London Borough of Lambeth

Luckock, B. (2007) 'Safeguarding children and integrated children's services', in Wilson, K. And James, A. (eds) (2007) *The Child Protection Handbook* (3rd edition), London: Baillière Tindall

McTernan, E. and Godfrey, A. (2006) 'Children's services planning in Northern Ireland: developing a planning model to address rights and needs', *Child Care in Practice*, Vol. 12, No. 3, pp. 219–40

Moore, C. (1996) *The Kincora Scandal: Political Cover-up and Intrigue in Northern Ireland*, Dublin: Marino Books

Murray, K., and Hill, M. (1991) 'The recent history of Scottish child welfare', *Children and Society*, Vol.15, No. 3, pp. 2666–81

National Assembly for Wales (2003) *Response to Serious Concern about Local Authority Social Services*, Cardiff: National Assembly for Wales

National Assembly for Wales (2006) *Keeping Us Safe: Report of the Safeguarding Vulnerable Children Review*

National Safeguarding Delivery Unit (2009) *Interim Progress Report and Work Programme 2009–2010*, London: Department for Children, Schools and Families

Northern Ireland Sex Offender Strategic Management Committee (2008) *Case Review on the Inter-agency Handling of Arthur McElhill as a Registered Sex Offender*, Belfast: NISOSMC

O'Brien, M., Bachmann, M., Husbands, C. *et al.* (2006) 'Integrating children's services to promote children's welfare: early findings from the implementation of Children's Trusts in England', *Child Abuse Review*, Vol. 15, pp. 377–95

Office for National Statistics (2009) 'Proportion of UK-born population aged under 16' (online). Available from URL: www.statistics.gov.uk/CCI/nugget.asp?ID=2192&Pos=2&ColRank=2&Rank=224 (accessed 1 December 2009)

Office of the First Minister and Deputy First Minister (2006) *Our Children – Our Pledge: A Ten Year Strategy for Children and Young People in Northern Ireland 2006–2016*, Belfast: OFMDFM

Owen, H. (2009) 'From protection to safeguarding: bringing you up to date on statutory responsibilities', in Hughes, L. and Owen, H. (eds) (2009) *Good Practice in Safeguarding Children*, London: Jessica Kingsley

Parton, N. (1991) *Governing the Family: Child Care, Child Protection and the State*, Basingstoke: Macmillan

Parton, N. (1997) *Child Protection and Family Support: Tensions, Contradictions and Possibilities*, London: Routledge

Parton, N. (2006) *Safeguarding Childhood: Early Intervention and Surveillance in a Late Modern Society*, Basingstoke: Palgrave Macmillan

Parton, N. (2008) 'The "Change for Children" programme in England: towards the "preventive-surveillance" state', *Journal of Law and Society*, Vol. 35, No. 1, pp. 166–87

Peckover, S., White, S. and Hall, C. (2009) 'From policy to practice: implementation and negotiation of technologies in everyday child welfare', *Children and Society*, Vol. 23, No. 2, pp. 136–48

Pinkerton, J. and Campbell, J. (2002) 'Social work and social justice in Northern Ireland: towards a new occupational space', *British Journal of Social Work*, Vol. 32, No. 6, pp. 723–37

Pithouse, A. [forthcoming] 'Devolution and change since the Children Act 1989: new directions in Wales', *Journal of Children's Services* [accepted for publication]

Powell, F. (1982) 'Justice and the young offender in Northern Ireland', *British Journal of Social Work*, Vol. 12, No. 6, pp. 565–86

Powell, M. (ed.) (2008) *Modernising the Welfare State: The Blair Legacy*, Bristol: Policy Press

Rose, W. (2009) 'The assessment framework', in Horwath, J. (ed.) (2009) *The Child's World* (2nd edition), London: Jessica Kingsley

Sandford, M. (2005) 'Devolution is a process not a policy: the new governance of the English regions', ESRC (online). Available from URL: www.devolution.ac.uk/pdfdata/Briefing%2018%20-%20Sandford.pdf (accessed 23 February 2010)

Scottish Executive (2002) *'It's Everyone's Job to make sure I'm Alright': Report of the Child Protection Audit and Review*, Edinburgh: Scottish Executive

Scottish Executive (2004 [1964]) *The Kilbrandon Report: Report of the Committee on Children and Young Persons, Scotland* (re-issue), Edinburgh: Scottish Executive

Scottish Executive (2004a) *Protecting Children and Young People: The Charter*, Edinburgh: Scottish Executive

Scottish Executive (2004b) *Protecting Children and Young People: Framework for Standards*, Edinburgh: Scottish Executive

Scottish Executive (2004c) *Review of Children's Hearings System*, Edinburgh: Scottish Executive

Scottish Executive (2005) *Protecting Children and Young People: Child Protection Committees*, Edinburgh: Scottish Executive

Scottish Executive (2006) *Getting it Right for Every Child: Implementation Plan*, Edinburgh: Scottish Executive

Scottish Executive (2007) *Protection of Vulnerable Groups (Scotland) Act 2007: Scottish Vetting and Barring Scheme*, Edinburgh: Scottish Executive

Scottish Government (2007) *The Scottish Budget Spending Review*, Edinburgh: Scottish Government

Scottish Government (2008) *A Guide to Getting it Right for Every Child*, Edinburgh: Scottish Government

Scottish Government (2009) *Your Scotland, Your Voice: A National Conversation*, Edinburgh: Scottish Government

Scottish Office (1995) *Children (Scotland) Act 1995*, Edinburgh: Scottish Office

Scottish Office (1998) *Protecting Children – A Shared Responsibility: Guidance on Inter-agency Co-operation*, Edinburgh: The Stationery Office

Scottish Parliament (2006) *The Joint Inspection of Children's Services and Inspection of Social Work Services (Scotland) Act 2006*, Edinburgh: Scottish Parliament

Secretary of State for Social Services (1974) *Report of the Committee of Inquiry into the Care and Supervision Provided in Relation to Maria Colwell*, London: HMSO

Secretary of State for Social Services (1988) *Report of the Inquiry into Child Abuse in Cleveland*, Cmd 3703, London: HMSO

Sidebotham, P. and Weeks, M. (2010) 'Multidisciplinary contributions to assessment of children in need', in J. Horwath (ed.) (2009) *The Child's World* (2nd edition), London: Jessica Kingsley

Social Work Services Group (1975) *Non Accidental Injury to Children*, Circular 1975, Edinburgh: Scottish Office

Social Work Task Force (2009) *Building a Safe, Confident Future: The Final Report of the Social Work Task Force*, London: Department of Children, Schools and Families

Spratt, T. (2000) 'Decision making by senior social workers at point of first referral', *British Journal of Social Work*, Vol. 30, No. 5, pp. 597–618

Stafford, A. and Vincent, S. (2008) *Safeguarding and Protecting Children and Young People*, Edinburgh: Dunedin Academic Press

Staffordshire County Council (1991) *The Pindown Experience and the Protection of Children*, Stafford: Staffordshire County Council

Stradling, B., MacNeil, M. and Berry, H. (2009) *Changing Professional Practice and Culture to Get it Right for Every Child. An Evaluation of the Early Development Phases of Getting it Right for Every Child in Highland: 2006–2009*, Edinburgh: Scottish Government

Tarara, H. and Daniel, B. (2007) *Audit of Scottish Child Care and Protection Research*, Edinburgh: Children in Scotland

Utting, W. (1991) *Children in the Public Care: A Review of Residential Child Care*, London: HMSO

Utting, W. (1997) *People Like Us: The Report of the Review of the Safeguards for Children Living Away from Home* (the Utting Report), London: The Stationery Office

Vincent, S. (2008a) *Inter-agency Guidance in Relation to Child Protection: A UK Comparison*, Briefing No. 2, June 2008, The University of Edinburgh/NSPCC Centre for UK-wide Learning in Child Protection (CLiCP)

Vincent, S. (2008b) *Mechanisms for the Strategic Implementation, Development and Monitoring of Inter-agency Child Protection Policy and Practice in the UK: The Role of Local Safeguarding Children Boards (LSCBs) and (Area) Child Protection Committees ((A)CPCs)*, Briefing No. 4, November 2008, The University of Edinburgh/NSPCC Centre for UK-wide Learning in Child Protection (CLiCP)

Vincent, S. (2009) 'The role of child protection committees in Scotland', *Exchange*, Issue 9 (Spring), London: NSPCC

Waterhouse, R. (2000) *Lost in Care: Report of the Tribunal of Inquiry into the Abuse of Children in Care in the Former Council Areas of Gwynedd and Clwyd since 1974*, HC201, London: The Stationery Office

Welsh Assembly Government (2004) *Children and Young People: Rights to Action*, Cardiff: Welsh Assembly Government

Welsh Assembly Government (2006a) *Beyond Boundaries: Citizen-Centred Local Services for Wales*, Cardiff: Welsh Assembly Government

Welsh Assembly Government (2006b) *Making the Connections – Delivering Beyond Boundaries*, Cardiff: Welsh Assembly Government

Welsh Assembly Government (2006c) *Safeguarding Children: Working Together Under the Children Act 2004*, Cardiff: Welsh Assembly Government

Welsh Assembly Government (2007a) *Designed for Life*, Cardiff: Welsh Assembly Government

Welsh Assembly Government (2007b) *Fulfilled Lives, Supportive Communities*, Cardiff: Welsh Assembly Government

Welsh Assembly Government (2009a) *NHS in Wales: Why We Are Changing the Structure*, Cardiff: Welsh Assembly Government

Welsh Assembly Government (2009b) *Statutory Guidance on the Role and Accountabilities of the Director of Social Services*, Cardiff: Welsh Assembly Government.

Western and Eastern Health and Social Services Boards (2007) *The Report of the Independent Inquiry Panel into the Deaths of Madeleine and Lauren O'Neill*, Belfast: Eastern Health and Social Services Board

Index

Note: page numbers in *italics* denote figures
or tables

abuse: access to children 50–1; deaths from
13–14, 58–9, 62, 64, 79–80; defined 10, 50;
DHSS circulars 12–13; extra-familial/intra-
familial 15; ritual/organised/institutional
15, 48–9; statistics 24–5; *see also* emotional
abuse; physical abuse; sexual abuse
An Abuse of Trust 51
access to children 9, 50–1, 65
accountability: central government/public
sector 69; Child Protection Committees
7, 75; directors of social services 37, 40;
GIRFEC 69; HMIE 71; increased 64;
inter-agency 4; *Laming Report* 6, 69; local
authorities 43; Local Safeguarding Children
Boards 11; partnership 20–1; professional
64; public 73
adult perpetrators/child safety 65; *see also* sex
offenders
All Wales Child Protection Procedures 5, 41,
80
Anglo-Irish Treaty (1921) 46
Annual Report for Social Service in Wales 43
Area Child Protection Committees 4, 6, 11,
13, 40, 50, 54
Area Review Committees 13, 50
Area Safeguarding Children's Boards 80
Assembly Measures 32–3
assessment 8–9, *25*, 55–6, 70, 73
assessment frameworks 9, 11, 17–18; *see also*
integrated assessment frameworks
asylum-seekers' children 65
Audit and Review of Child Protection 67, 68,
71–4
Audit Commission 14
Ayre, P. 59

Baby Peter: *see* Connelly, Peter
Balls, Ed 27, 29
Beckford, Jasmine 13
Beecham, Jeremy 33–4
Belfast Agreement 60
Belfast Telegraph 59
Black Report 48

Blair, Tony 16
Bradley, D. 59
Brent 13
Brown, A. 65
Buckley, H. 56
Bulger, James 27
bureaucratic factors 26, 53

Campbell, J. 47
Care and Social Services Inspectorate Wales
35, 41, 42, 43–4
care homes: *see* residential homes
care needs/service users 28, 36
Carlile, Kimberley 13
Centre for Learning in Child Protection
(CLiCP) xii–xiii, 77
Change Co-ordinator 54
*Chief Inspector's: Annual Report for Social
Service in Wales* 43
Chief Secretary to the Treasury 19, 21–2
child abuse: *see* abuse
Child Assessment Order 9
child care policy, NI 47
child death review panels 4, 23
child deaths 13–14, 58–9, 62, 64, 79–80; *see
also specific cases*
child poverty 60
child protection: bureaucracy 26, 53;
and child welfare 24, 78; Children Act
(1989) 17; England xiii, 12–30; forensic
investigative model 10; guidance 5, 23;
inspection 43–4, 51–3, 58, 71–4, 76;
international comparisons 78; Northern
Ireland xiv, 2, 11, 45–61; and prevention
19; procedures 7–10, 51; professionalisation
29, 30, 50; safeguarding 18–19, 22–3;
scandals 13, 48–9, 63–4; Scotland xiii,
62–76; and social exclusion 6–17, 22; UK
wide 1, 3; Wales xiii–xiv, 31–44; *see also*
Laming Report
Child Protection: Messages from Research
(DoH) 14
child protection case conference 9, 10
Child Protection Committees 7, 11, 73, 74–5
Child Protection Orders 8
Child Protection Panels 6–7

child protection plans *25*; Baby Peter 28; children at risk 14; emotional abuse 25; neglect 25; physical abuse 26; procedures 9–10; sexual abuse 26

Child Protection Reform Programme 3, 7, 62, 74

Child Protection Register: child protection plan 9, 13; decision-making 9–10; Haringey 28; HMIE 74; Northern Ireland 10, 57; reduction in names 71; and referrals 14, 71

child safety 65, 75

child welfare: and child protection 24, 78; funding for 60; guidance 23; legislation 3–5; Northern Ireland 46; policies 1–2; Scotland 63

child-centred approach 4, 44

Children, Schools and Families Commons Committee 28

Children Act (1989) 4, 11, 14–15, 17, 20

Children Act (2004): accountability/partnership 20–1; agencies working with children 4; children and young people's partnerships 40; Local Safeguarding Children Boards 11; statutory duties 5, 23; Wales 4, 5, 6, 34–6

Children and Families (Wales) Measure 33

Children and Family Court Advisory and Support Service 28

Children and Young People: Rights to Action in Wales 2

Children and Young People - Our Pledge 2, 3

Children and Young People's Framework Partnerships 6

children and young people's partnerships 36–7, 40

Children and Young People's Plan 6, 21

Children and Young People's Rights to Action 3

Children and Young Person's Act (1950) 46

Children and Young Person's Act (2008) 23

Children and Young Person's Act (Northern Ireland) (1968) 46

children at risk 11, 14, 75; *see also* vulnerable children

children in care 15; *see also* residential homes

children in need 4, 11, 14–15

Children (Northern Ireland) Order (1995) 4, 51, 58

Children (Scotland) Act (1995) 4, 64

Children's and Young People's Unit 16

Children's Charter 68

Children's Commissioner 21

Children's Hearing Review 69

Children's Hearing System xiv, 7, 63, 68–9, 75–6, 78

Children's Hearings Bill, Draft 63

Children's Reporter 7, 8, 71, 73

children's rights movement 16; *see also* rights of children

children's services 2, 4–6, 37–8, 77; *see also* children's social care

Children's Services Bill (2006) 4–6

Children's Services Plan 6, 7

children's social care 5, 28, 31–2

Children's Trust 5, 6, 11, 20–1

Cleveland affair 14, 64

CLiCP (Centre for Learning in Child Protection) xii–xiii, 77

Climbié, Victoria Adjo 19, 28, 34, 51–2, 58–9

Clyde, Lord 64

collaboration/devolution 81

Colwell, Maria 12, 13, 47, 64

Community Planning Partnerships 67

community policing 72

community-based social services 47

computer use 22; *see also* information communication technology; internet

Concordat in Scotland 5, 66, 80

confidentiality issues 58, 70

Connelly, Peter (Baby Peter) 26–9; aftermath of death xiii, 35, 79; child protection plan 28; errors made 30; Joint Area Review 34; media coverage 29; policy changes 12; public uproar 58

consent issues 58, 69

ContactPoint 20, 29, 81

Convention of Scottish Local Authorities (COSLA) 80

Cooper, A. xiii, 59, 77

Co-operating to Protect Children (HSS/CC) 50

Co-operating to Safeguard Children (Department of Health, Social Services and Public Safety) 5, 51

cooperation: GIRFEC 70; interagency 20–1, 50; lack of 13

Corbett, J. xiii

Corby, B. 13

COSLA (Convention of Scottish Local Authorities) 80

criminal justice systems approach 78

Curtis Report 46

Daily Mirror 27

Daniel, B. 62

day-care settings 15

deaths from child abuse: *see* child deaths

decentralisation 80

Department for Children, Schools and

Families *25*
Department for Education and Skills 19
Department of Health: *Child Protection: Messages from Research* 14, 51; *Framework for the Assessment of Children in Need and their Families* 9, 17–18, 24; inquiries into child deaths 13, 14; lack of coordination noted 50; local authority social services 15; reports on implementation 14; *Safeguarding Children* 2; UNOCINI 56; *Working Together to Safeguard Children* 17–18
Department of Health, Social Services and Public Safety 5, 46, 49, 51, 52, 53, 55, 56–7, 58, 59
Department of Health and Social Security 12–13, 50, 64
Department of Health and Social Services 48, 49, 50
deprivation 46, 48
Designed for Life (Welsh Assembly Government) 33
Devaney, J. xiv, 52, 60, 80
devolution: child protection systems 79; and collaboration 81; policy development xii, xiv, 60–1, 62, 77, 80; Scotland 65; Wales 31, 32
direct rule 47, 60
Director of Children's Services 5, 6, 20, 27
Director of Social Services 6, 36, 37–40
Directors of Social Work 7
discrimination/social housing 47
diversity, valuing 70
drug squads 72
Dunblane shootings 64–5

Eames, R. 59
eCare system 81
Economic Research Institute for Northern Ireland 60
e-documentation 57
Education Act (1996) 27
education departments 5
education in personal safety 73
e-government strategy 22
emergency action 8
Emergency Protection Orders 8
emotional abuse 10, 24, 25
emotional neglect 14
England: child deaths 62; child protection xiii, 12–30; Children Act (2004) 4; Children and Young People's Plan 6; Children's Trust 5, 6, 11, 20–1; Common Assessment Framework 9; Director of Children's Services 5; *Framework for the Assessment of Children in Need and their Families* 9,

17–18, 24; Integrated Children's System 9, 28–9; local authorities 5, 24; Ofsted inspections 21, 27, 29, 71; safeguarding 75; social care, adult/children 31–2; *see also Every Child Matters*
Estyn 42
Evason, E. 48
Every Child Matters: Change for Children 19–26; Baby Peter 26, 29; child-centred outcomes-led approach 4; England/Ireland 3; *Laming Report* 2, 28; outcomes 3; reforms xiii, 3
Every Child Matters Green Paper 19, 21–2
Exclusion Orders 8

Facebook groups 29
failure to thrive, non-organic 10
family life/intervention 64
family protection units 72
family support: Children Act (1989) 14–15; New Labour 16; Northern Ireland 60; universal services 78–9; UNOCINI 56, 57; Wales 33
Featherstone, B. 16
fit for purpose systems 22, 28
forensic investigative model 10
fostering service 46
Framework for Standards, Scottish Executive 68
Framework for the Assessment of Children in Need and their Families (DoH) 9, 17–18, 24
France, A. 21
Franklin, B. 27
Frost, N. 2, 4, 9, 11, 22
Fulfilled Lives, Supporting Communities (Welsh Assembly Government) 33

Gateway Teams 55, 57
Getting it Right for Every Child (GIRFEC) framework 68–71; Children's Services Bill 4–6; core components 69–70; development of xiv, 75–6, 80; Lead Professional 70; learning from English experiences 81; national audit 2–3, 67; Scottish Executive 2–3; Scottish Government 2, 3, 69; Scottish Nationalist Party 5; service delivery 69; shared approach 69; support network 71; values and principles 62, 70–1; well-being in children 69–71
Gilbert, N. 78
GIRFEC: *see Getting it Right for Every Child* framework
Godfrey, A. 51
Government of Wales Act (1998) 31, 32
Government of Wales Act (2006) 32, 33
Greenwich 13

Guardian 27
guidance: assessment frameworks 9;
    child protection 5, 23; Child Protection
    Committees 68; child welfare 23;
    interagency 7, 10; and legislation 7;
    statutory/non-statutory 5, 23; Welsh
    Assembly Government 38–9

Hammond review 67
Haringey 26–9
Hayes, D. 52
Health and Social Care Board 53
Health and Social Care Trusts 54, 55
Health and Social Services Boards 6–7, 47
Health and Social Services Trusts 52, 53
Health Inspectorate Wales 42
Healthcare Commission 27
Hendrick, H. 46
Henry, Tyra 13
Her Majesty's Inspectorate of Education: *see*
    HMIE
Highland Region, Pathfinder project 71
Hill, M. xiii, 64, 77, 78
Hillyard, P. 60
HM Government 2, 5, 18–19, 22, 23–4, 30
HMI Constabulary 42
HMI Probation 42
HMIE (Her Majesty's Inspectorate of
    Education) 71–4; accountability 71; *How
    Well are Children Protected and Their
    Needs Met?* 72; *How Well Do We Protect
    Children and Meet their Needs?* 74; *National
    Performance Framework* 73–4; quality
    indicators 72, 74
Home Office 17
Horwath, J. 42, 56
House of Commons, Northern Ireland 46
*How Well are Children Protected and Their
    Needs Met?* (HMIE) 72
*How Well Do We Protect Children and Meet
    their Needs?* (HMIE) 74
Howarth, Jan 41
Hudson, B. 19, 42
Hughes Report 49
human rights 58
Huston, Martin 50

Implementation Group 54
information communication technology 22,
    26, 28–9
information sharing 69, 70, 75
Ingleby Report 46
in-service training 50
inspection of child protection services 43–4,
    51–3, 58, 71–4
integrated assessment frameworks 11

Integrated Children's System 9, 28–9
integration 20–1, 31
interagency working 5, 67–8; *see also*
    cooperation; integration
internet/child safety 65, 75
intervention: early stages 3, 11, 20, 22, 78;
    family life 64; legislation 7, 8; significant
    harm 23; thresholds for 78
interventionist approach 64
intra-country comparative work xiii, 78

Joint Area Review 27, 34
Joint Inspection of Children's Services
    (Scotland) Act (2006) 68, 72
juvenile delinquency 47, 63

Keeping Us Safe (National Assembly for
    Wales) 2
Kilbrandon Committee 63
Kincora Boys' Home 48–9, 50
Kirton, D. 47
Knight, C. xiv
Kouao, Marie Therese 19

Labour and Plaid Cymru Groups 32
Labour Party 32; *see also* New Labour
Laing, R. D. xiii, 77
Lambeth 13
Laming, Lord 19, 27, 52
Laming Report 2, 5, 6, 19, 28, 29–30, 34, 35
Lead Councillor 5, 20
lead director 37–8
Lead Professional, GIRFEC 70
legislation 3–5, 7, 8
Lindon, J. 3, 10
local authorities: accountability 43; children
    and young people's partnerships 36–7;
    Children and Young People's Plan 21;
    children's social care 7, 8; England 5, 24;
    Scotland 7, 72; social services departments
    17; Social Work Services Group 64; Wales
    32, 33, 35, 43
Local Authorities Social Services Act (1970)
    18
Local Government Association 28
Local Health Boards 32
Local Safeguarding Children Boards:
    Haringey 29; reviews 35; statutory 4, 6, 11,
    20, 23; Wales 5, 40–2
Local Safeguarding Panels 54
Luckock, B. 4, 10, 11

McAndrew, F. xiv, 80
McElhill, Arthur 59
McFarlane, Kennedy 67
McGovern, Lorraine, and children 59

McGrath, William 48
McTernan, E. 51
Making the Connections -- Delivering Beyond Boundaries (Welsh Assembly Government) 33–4
Manning, Carl 19
Maria Colwell Inquiry 13, 64
media reporting xiii, 26–7, 29, 43, 59
mental illness, parents 17, 57
Merseyside sexual abuse allegations 15
Moore, C. 48
Morrison, Tony 41
Muir, Brandon 79–80
Murray, K. 64
My World Triangle 9, 71

National Assembly for Wales 2, 32–3, 37–8; *see also* Welsh Assembly Government
National Child Protection Guidance 76
National Conversation, Scottish Government 66
National Health Service reforms 32
National Health Service Trusts 32
national outcomes 3
National Performance Framework 67, 73–4
National Safeguarding Delivery Unit 35
needs, vulnerable children 56–7, 67, 72–3, 76
neglect 10, 14, 24, 25, 50, 64
New Labour 15, 16–19
North South Ministerial Council 60
Northern Ireland: audit of child protection services 52; *Black Report* 48; child care policy 47; child poverty 60; child protection xiv, 2, 11, 45–61; Child Protection Panels 6–7; Child Protection Register 10, 57; child welfare 46; child welfare services 46, 60; *Children and Young People – Our Pledge* 2, 3; Children and Young Person's Act (1950) 46; Children (Northern Ireland) Order (1995) 4, 51, 58; *Co-operating to Safeguard Children* 5, 58; direct rule 47, 60; family support 60; government resignation 47; Health and Social Services Boards 6–7, 47; House of Commons 46; inspection of child protection services 51–3, 58; interagency coherence 52; Office of the First Minister and Deputy First Minister 2; population 45; public service agencies 47, 80; Reform Implementation Team 54–5, 57–8; residential homes 49, 53; Review of Public Administration 53–5; Safeguarding Board 4, 7, 54; social services referral 8; social/political changes 45; troubles 47, 59; UNOCINI 9, 55–7
Northern Ireland Act (1998) 60

Northern Ireland Assembly 49, 80
Northern Ireland Commissioner for Children and Young People 53
Northern Ireland Parliament 46
Northern Ireland Sex Offender Strategic Management Committee 59
Noyes, P. xiii, 79
NSPCC 8, 19, 57

O'Brien, M. 6
Office for National Statistics 45
Office for Standards in Education (Ofsted) 21, 71, 27, 29
Office of the First Minister and Deputy First Minister, Northern Ireland 2
Ofsted 21, 27, 29, 71
One Wales 32
O'Neill, Lauren 58–9
O'Neill, Madeleine 58–9
Orkney Report 64
Owen, H. 4

Panorama 29
parents: of juvenile delinquents 63; mental illness 17, 57; poor skills 22; refusal of access to child 9; role of 16; and social workers 51; substance misuse 10, 17, 57, 75; support for 36–7, 51
partnership 20–1, 36–7, 40, 42–3
Parton, N. xiii, 2, 4, 9, 11, 14, 20, 22, 79
Pathfinder project, Highland Region 71
Peckover, S. 22
performance-management approach 26
personal safety education 73
Petley, J. 27
physical abuse 10, 24, 26, 48, 64
Pindown 15
Pinkerton, J. 47
Pithouse, A. 32, 34–5, 41
Plaid Cymru 32
police inspectorate 27
police protection powers 8
political consensus 29
Poor Law provisions 46
Powell, F. 47
Powell, M. 16
pregnancy, neglect during 10
prevention 19; child protection 19; deprivation 46; early intervention 3, 78; increasing focus on 79; public health approach 21; risk and protection 21; social exclusion 22
Prior, James 49
procedures 7–10, 51
professional dialogue 73
professionalisation 29, 30, 50

Project Reference Group 54
prostitution 10
Protecting Children -- a Shared Responsibility
   (Scottish Office) 5, 75
The Protection of Children in England: see
   Laming Report
Protection of Vulnerable Groups (Scotland)
   Act (2007) 65
public action, children at risk 75
public health approach 21
public service agencies, Northern Ireland 47,
   80

Red Dragon 43
referrals 25; Children's Hearings 7; electronic
   57; falling rates 71; Gateway Teams 55, 57;
   statutory services 8; by telephone 8
Reform Implementation Team 54–5, 57–8
Reid, C. 60
Report of the Care of Children Committee 46
Report of the Committee on Children and
   Young People 1960 46
Report of the Committee on Local Authority
   and Allied Personal Social Services 46–7
residential homes: abuse 15, 48–9; Northern
   Ireland 49, 53; safety of children 64; staff
   training 46
Resilience Matrix 71
Review of Public Administration 53–5
rights of children 3, 16, 58, 64, 67
rights-based approach 34
risk assessment 73, 75
risk factors 21–2
Rodgers, T. xiv, 80
Rose, W. xiii, 4, 9, 11, 24, 79
runaway children 74

safe havens 65
safeguarding 18–19, 22–3; child protection
   18–19, 22–3; Children Act (1989) 17;
   as concept 11, 15; England 75; local
   authorities in Wales 35; welfare promotion
   26, 30; Welsh Assembly Government 31;
   workforce development 42
Safeguarding Board 4, 7, 54
Safeguarding Children: A Joint Chief
   Inspectors' Report (DoH) 2
Safeguarding Children: Working Together
   under the Children Act 2004 (Welsh
   Assembly Government) 5, 35, 41
Safeguarding Children Boards 41
Safeguards Review 15
Sandford, M. 65
scandals 13, 48–9, 63–4
Scotland xiii, 62–76; *Audit and Review of*
   Child Protection 67; central and local

government 5, 80; child deaths 64; child
   protection xiii, 7, 62–76; Child Protection
   Committees 7, 11; Child Protection Orders
   8; Child Protection Register 10; child
   welfare 63; Children (Scotland) Act (1995)
   4; Children's Hearing System; children's
   services plan 7; devolution 65; Directors
   of Social Work 7; economic downturn 66;
   inspection and regulatory changes 71–4;
   local authorities 7, 72; *My World Triangle*
   9, 71; national outcomes 3; socio-politics
   of 65, 66–7, 80; *see also* Children's Hearing
   System
Scotland Budget Spending Review 66–7
Scottish Executive: Child Protection Reform
   Programme 7; child protection system xiii;
   Children's Charter 68; *Children's Hearing*
   Review 69; delinquency 63; Framework
   for Standards 68; GIRFEC framework 2–3;
   Guidance to Child Protection Committees
   68; Hammond review 67; safe havens 65
Scottish Government: Child Protection
   Committees 74–5; Community Planning
   Partnerships 67; GIRFEC 2, 3, 69; National
   Conversation 66; public sector 66–7;
   statutory/non-statutory guidance 5
Scottish Nationalist Party 5, 66, 71, 80
Scottish Office 5, 64, 65, 75
Secretary of State for Northern Ireland 47
Secretary of State for Social Services 12, 14,
   47
Seebohm Report 46–7
self-evaluation 73
Serious Case Reviews 23, 27, 29, 35, 43, 81
serious concern protocol 38
service delivery 33–4, 57–8, 69
service users/care needs 36
sex offenders 50–1, 59, 60
sexual abuse: awareness of 64; children
   in care 15; decline 24, 26; defined 10;
   Kincora Boys' Home 48; perpetrators
   50–1, 59, 60; suspected 14
Shoesmith, Sharon 27
Sidebotham, P. 42
significant harm: assessment 8–9; defined
   4, 7, 17–18; intervention 23; Local
   Safeguarding Children Boards 40; Social
   Work (Scotland) Act (1968) 63
Single Outcome Agreement process 66–7
social care, adult/children 5, 28, 31–2
social exclusion 16–17, 22
social housing 47
social services: community-based 47; as lead
   agency 13; local authorities 17; referral 8;
   Wales 31, 36–7
social work departments 8, 42, 63–4

Social Work (Scotland) Act (1968) 63
Social Work Services Group 64
Social Work Task Force 27, 29, 30, 35, 55
social workers: assessed year in employment 55; coordinating child protection 13; development 42; and parents 51; pressures on 28, 29–30; professionalism 29, 30; recruitment 28; undergraduate training 57; Wales 42
Soham murders 65
Spratt, T. 52
staff training 46
Stafford, A. xiv, 3, 5, 7, 63, 78
Staffordshire children's homes 15
Staffordshire County Council 15
Stradling, B. 71
structural reform of services 67–8
substance misuse, parents 10, 17, 57, 75
Sun 27, 29
Swansea Sound 43

Tara paramilitaries 48
Tarara, H. 62
telephone referrals 8
Tierney, M. xiv
trafficked children 74

Understanding the Needs of Children in Northern Ireland (UNOCINI) 9, 55–7
United Nations Convention of the Rights of the Child 3, 34, 51, 56
UNOCINI (*Understanding the Needs of Children in Northern Ireland*) 9, 55–7
Utting, D. 21
Utting, W. 15, 49

Victoria Climbié Inquiry 34
Vincent, S. xiii, 3, 5, 6, 7, 10, 11, 34, 41, 63, 78
violence: domestic 17, 57; paramilitary 47
voluntary organisations 51
vulnerable children 33, 67–8, 76; needs 56–7, 67, 72–3, 76
Vulnerable Children Measure 33

waiting list cases 53
Wales xiii–xiv, 31–44; child protection xiii–xiv, 31–44; child-centred approach 44; Children Act (2004) 4, 5, 6, 34–6;

Children and Young People: Rights to Action in Wales 2; Children and Young People's Framework Partnerships 6; Children and Young People's Plan 6; devolution 31, 32; Director of Social Services 6, 37–40; family support 33; *Framework for the Assessment of Children in Need and their Families* 9; Health Inspectorate 42; Integrated Children's System 9; Labour Party 32; *Laming Report* 34; local authorities 32, 33, 35, 43; Local Safeguarding Children Boards 5, 40–2; media reporting 43; National Health Service reforms 32; *One Wales* 32; partnership 42–3; population 32; sexual abuse allegations 15; social services 31, 36–7; social workers 42; welfare promotion 36; *Young People's Rights to Action* 3; *see also* National Assembly for Wales; Welsh Assembly Government
Wales Audit Office 42
Waterhouse, R. 15
Weeks, M. 42
welfare committees 46
welfare promotion 18, 22, 26, 30, 36
well-being in children 69–71
Welsh Assembly Government xiv, 2; *Designed for Life* 33; *Fulfilled Lives, Supporting Communities* 33; guidance 38–9; inspectorates 43–4; *Making the Connections – Delivering Beyond Boundaries* 33–4; NHS reforms 32; safeguarding 31; *Safeguarding Children* 5, 35, 41; and Welsh Local Government Association 38; *see also* National Assembly for Wales
Welsh Local Government Association 38
Welsh Office 50
Western and Eastern Health and Social Services Boards 58
Whelan, S. 56
whole-child approach 70
workhouses 46
Working Together to Safeguard Children (HM Government/DoH) 5, 17, 18–19, 23–4, 30, 51
Working Together Under the Children Act 1989 (Home Office) 17

Young People's Rights to Action 3